THE CHOICE

Professional Networker or Corporate Executive

Two Career Paths to Dreams, Riches, Time, Comfort & Family

Dr Teng Heng Chan

Foreword

Nobody told me there was an alternative to earning a living.

The conventional way was to study hard, get a university degree, get a job, and you had it made.

The truth was further than many realized.

This tells in a story book form the path two persons took to discover their dreams, riches, time for themselves and their families and final comfort for the rest of their lives.

The professional networker and the corporate executive. The latter working hard to climb up the corporate ladder, while the professional networking works hard to the top level to earn the money and the dream.

There are similarities between the two, in that there are dreams, goals, hard work, payout, realities hitting hard and review of the dreams and goals. The stories of the choices one makes are based on real experiences. Some have made it, and some have not. However, the stories relate how one can achieve dreams and goals, if the path and motivation is right.

To my wife Yvonne, children Rachael and Westley, the discovery in our lifetime of an alternative to earn a living was worth the quest and search stretching over 4 decades.

To my mentors, thank you for your wisdom, whether in the corporate world or in the professional network marketing world.

Table of Contents

Foreward
1	The Professional Networker / The Corporate Executive	5
2	The Beginning	7
3	The Novelty Effect Wears Off	11
4	Reality Hits Hard	18
5	Facts I, Facts II, Facts III	20
6	The Referral Network & The Corporate Network	33
7	Choice I, Choice II	39
8	Talk With The Wife	45
9	How Does It Work	49
10	The Dream	53
11	The 100 Goals	57
12	List	61
13	Invitations	65
14	Show the Plan I, II	69
15	Doing the Work I, II	71
16	How Money is Made	77
17	Personal Development	81
18	First Payout	85
19	Counselling I, II	89
20	Leading a Team	97
21	Cost-Benefit Analysis	101
22	Emotional Roller Coasting	105
23	The Next Level	109
24	Self Affirmation	113
25	Preparation	117
26	Reasons	121
27	Action Time, or Is It?	125
28	7 Logical Reasons	129
29	7 Emotional Reasons	132
30	Key Success Factors	135

31 In The Thick of IT I, II	139
32 What Is My Priority ?	147
33 Clash of Priorities	151
34 The System Works	155
35 Core Group	159
36 One-Quit	163
37 The Search Begins	167
38 Going Emerald / Going For Top 5	171
39 Real People, Real Scenario, Behind The Stories	173

1 The Professional Networker

This is Tom who realized that he had only 24 hours a day, and only 4 hours of discretionary time to pursue what he wanted to do.

He could leverage his time by building a group of like-minded persons who would pursue the same dreams as he has

- to be financially free, so that he does not need to worry about money.
- to be time free, so that he does not have to be shackled 9 to 5 to a job
- to be able to spend time with his family, especially his children
- to be able to live comfortably with his childhood friend who is now his wife
- to be able to travel and see the world
- to work on projects he loves, such as raising funds the needy students
- to donate to just causes

If he could find a vehicle which would generate the money by leveraging his discretionary time, he could fulfil his dreams.

1 The Corporate Executive

This is Peter who has read about the CEOs who earn megabucks. He would like to be one of them.

As corporate executive, he would

- be in absolute power to run his corporation as he likes
- command a handsome salary
- have all the perks, like company car and be chauffeur-driven all around town
- have a dream life-style, jetting around the world, staying in corporate-account suites or luxurious hotels
- be able to spend lavishly on company accounts
- have a nice office, with thick carpeting and timber-cladded office
- have an efficient and nice-looking secretary
- have a nice holiday paid for by his company
- have time for golf, and vacations, entertaining clients
- let his staff do all the work and he would be dining and wining clients

He knew he has to do it by being smart, suave, witty but at the same time politically intelligent

He must do it by the time he is in mid 30s and thereafter, its plain sailing.

His family well-being and wealth will depend on corporate stock options and bonuses.

His dream: to conquer the world by being a corporate warrior.

2 The Professional Networker ~ The Beginning

Tom has been working for a corporation for three years now, after graduating with a good Honors degree from a reputable university, having attained magna cum laude.

In his first year at work, he was really happy as now he has risen from "poverty class" as a student. He can now buy those "man" things he really longed for: the fastest computer he had been eyeing since his undergraduate days, the palm top that he deemed too expensive, and the suit that he could only looked at. Now with credit cards, a good salary, and a new car, what else could he wish for?

Never mind he had to work late; it's learning for him. Anyway, his fiancée, also works late in their first year. They go to work together and get time off together. So, the first year at work was a not snag.

Year two of his job saw him getting more responsibilities. As he was capable, his supervisor gave him more work. He really had a good first year, so his salary escalation was really satisfactory. No complaints there though. He now earns $36,000 gross. Not too bad. He got married that year end. His wife also had a good year. Now, they have to work later. Sometimes Tom had to stay back later, so his wife, Shirley, had to go back by herself first. Used to having meals together, now they are getting dinners on their own more frequently. They would however take supper together; simple snacks, sometimes sandwiches, sometimes, just plain tea and biscuits.

In the third year, Shirley was expecting their first baby. Boy, was Tom over the moon. He could not explain the experience...he never thought he would be a father so soon. He was very happy. Shirley was at first exhilarated. Then the morning sickness and the weight became a problem. Though she looked forward to being a mother,

she never thought it would be so challenging, especially when she was down with cravings for certain foods and Tom was not there to help her. "Him, and his work again!"

In the eight months of her pregnancy, Shirley was prepared for the rush to the delivery ward at the local hospital. Tom and she had a few trial runs, when they thought the baby was due. After a few false alarms, this is it. The cutest little baby was born. Alison was their charming little darling. Tom was the happiest father in the block. He started to arrange time at the office so that he could be with his family. "It's great to be a father!"

2   The Corporate Executive ~ The Beginning

Peter graduated top of his class and gathered all the Honors that was available. He was also the all-rounder who managed to get his "dream girl" in his class. A very sociable person, he was voted "the most likely person to succeed" in his year.

As a type A * person, he was always the go-getter. Because of his good interpersonal skills and his charming personality, he could always influence and steer any group he was in to his desired direction. In class, he was always the natural leader.

In the annual milk-rounds when companies visit the university campus to recruit students, he not only got four offers, but they were the best offers from the best companies. He chose, not a large company, but a medium-sized company that he could rise very quickly up the corporate ladder. As he held many societies post of president or chairman, he could command a very high starting salary of $50,000. Wow! He thought, "I am going places. CEO is far me".

He was on a very steady and close relationship with Elizabeth, who was a very attractive lady. She also managed to get a very good position as one of the many executive assistants to the President and Chief Executive of a very large "new-age" company that was into internet, servers and wireless communications. She was offered a more modest salary of $30,000, but there were many opportunities to learn. Both Peter and Elizabeth agreed that they would devote at least 5 years to their career before they would talk about marriage. They knew what it took to be at the top, and they were mentally prepared for the hard slog and learning to get to the top.

Peter worked in a petroleum company where the perks were very competitive so he did not begrudge the long hours he had to put into

the corporate planning. At times, he had to work overnight to get the forecasting of the financial figures right. Elizabeth sometimes would not get to see him for up to 36 hours, and then Peter would emerge with flowers, as an apology, followed by dinner. The first three years for both of them were hectic, interesting and challenging. They would compare notes about their work environment, their bosses and their companies.

Both were given corporate expense accounts, which they could not use as they were working late hours. Nevertheless, they caught up with each other during weekends, when they would swim and meet up with former classmates. Boy, were they enjoying life. Work hard and play hard.

3   The Professional Networker
~ The Novelty Effect Wears Off

Tom and Shirley spent whatever time they could get with their new baby, Alison. It was marvellous to have an offspring, a result of their love for each other. The baby was so-o-o adorable.

As the weeks passed, Tom found that his life pattern was changing. Instead of coming back to spend time with Shirley, he found that Alison was their newfound centre of attention. And he loved it. However, because Alison would wake up in the night for her feeds, or to demand a change in nappies, Tom lacked sleep, and sometimes he found himself overly tired. Shirley, on maternity leave, first felt very a pleasant change from her office routine. However, day after day facing the baby and having to wake up in the night, and then to take care of the baby in the day, Shirley started to feel tired and worn out. Especially on those nights when Tom had to work late. Weekends were something they both looked forward to. However, as time progressed, and with deadlines, Tom began to work late, and extended work over weekends. This upset Shirley for she needed Tom's company. As she spent more time with Alison, she felt her mental capacity descending to baby talk, and kept losing her sense of dressing. She was so busy looking after Alison and the household chores, she started to neglect grooming and dressing. At times when Tom came back late, Shirley was too tired to chat with Tom, and would doze off, leaving Tom with the baby. Tom was also tired, and sometimes, this led to small tiffs over who should do what. Shirley could not wait to go back to work again, but she and Tom could not decide who should take care of Alison.

They decided to have their first serious discussion since they married. Tom agreed that Shirley should go back to work to preserve her sanity and self-esteem. Shirley however was undecided whether

she should leave Alison in the care of total strangers in child-care centres. Tom also missed Alison and longed to be able to spend at least weekends with her. He was also worried that Alison would be alone without her parents during weekdays. Both Tom and Shirley were stuck. Finally, Shirley suggested that she work part-time, so that she can at least spend more time with her daughter than a stranger would with her daughter.

Tom thought about it and felt that this was the best solution. However, he was cautious as this meant Shirley would be on half-salary, and this means that the household income would decrease by at least a quarter. Does this mean that Tom would have to work harder to compensate?

4 The Corporate Executive
~ The Novelty Effect Wears Off

Peter and Elizabeth felt on top of the world. Their career plans in the corporate world were proceeding as they expected. Then came the crunch.

Peter's boss was promoted, thanks partly to Peter and his colleagues. They gave him a good farewell and he promised that he would visit them often, even hinted that perhaps they might join him in his new posting. A new boss would be coming next week Monday. All of Peter's colleagues were eager with expectation that the new boss would be as good and supportive as the former boss.

Monday came. Arnold was a tall, athletic guy, very good looking and was very likeable with girls. After the introductions were made, Arnold came down to business. He said that he hoped they would offer him the cooperation they had given their former boss, and said that he would similarly support them and enable them in their work. His door was always open, he told them. However, he told them that he was used to getting his ways, as he has always been proven right. To help them ease their way, he would be bringing his assistant of many years with him She has been an asset to him and knows what he wants without even him mentioning it. They work so well as a team that he hoped the rest of them could similarly sense what is wanted in the job. That would make the whole department move in the right direction easily. With a smile, he told them he would be seeing them individually over the next few days. His assistant, April, would be joining him as soon as she was back from leave.

April came in on Wednesday, and Peter and his colleagues gawked at her. Not only was she pretty, she was also very friendly, giving each person a nice smile and greeting. No wonder, Peter thought, Arnold brought her with him! Arnold called everybody in the department and introduced April to them. "She is in charge," he told everyone, and then said, "excuse us", before April joined him in his office. That stunned everyone. Peter appeared puzzled. His previous boss was very open, and everyone could approach him, and he knew what each one was doing, or had done, and therefore rewarded them accordingly.

Now, they have to go through April, to gain access to the boss, and she had the run of the office. "I hope this won't lead to complications, as my previous boss promised me that I will be promoted in half-a-years' time", Peter recalled. With that he went back to his desk with a big frown of puzzlement and anticipation.

4   The Professional Networker ~Reality Hits Hard

Tom sat down to calculate the total household income. He was earning $40,000 when April was expecting, and she was contributing half of the total income. Now with her working part time, their combined income would be $60,000. In addition to that, their household expenses have increased with Alison, and with additional medical care. Hmmm, this doesn't look good. "Already my time I have with the family is already bad; if I work extra to make up the income, it would make the quality time with the family worse! Hmm, what can I do?"

He thought of asking his boss for a raise, but that would not be practical, as the next cycle of pay increment would be half a year away. Moonlighting would only add another $10,000 extra, but that would take away whatever time he had with April and Alison.

"How come," Tom thought to himself, "when the more experienced I am, I have less time, and even less overall income? With one child, April and I have $20,000 less income? With two children, that would be impossible? I would have to work doubly hard…and that would mean less time for me to spend with my family?"

Tom had the first hard reality to hit him. He thought that what his father told him would come easily true. "Study hard, work hard, get a university degree, and get a good job, marry a nice girl, and you have made it", his father told him. He had a good Honors degree, a nice girl, and a nice job, but he has not made it…the income has reduced with the family, the bills have increased, and worse, he has less time. Hmm, something is not right. Did his father miss out anything?

He must consult his friend, Paul, who was his senior in college. Paul always knew which way to go, although he was always very busy even during college. He observed that Paul was often in discussion with his college mates, every time talking to a different person. Paul had made many appointments with Tom, but Tom was always busy with college work, and with Shirley, courting and working together on their assignments. Hence, Tom never managed to meet up with Paul.

"Now, what is Paul's telephone number?" Tom wondered, and went to fetch his Palm Pilot.

4   The Corporate Executive ~ Reality Hits Hard

Peter wanted to make an appointment with Arnold to discuss what plans he had for him, and also to find out whether his former boss mentioned his promotion. On the phone, Arnold told him that he would be tied up with his one-on-one meetings with all staff in his department, and that he could only see Peter next week. If there was anything urgent, Arnold suggested, perhaps April could meet up with him first.

"Well, I'll never…", Peter thought to himself. It's Arnold who will decide on his promotion, not April. But after thinking a while, he thought why not have a chat with April, after all, she was very approachable, and since she knew about the work habits of Arnold, perhaps he could prepare for the meeting next week.

April was really attractive. She had that lovely smile on the face befitting a model. She was also very pleasant and was a good listener. "Ah, you must be Peter; Arnold told me to expect you," as perfume filled the room she occupied. "Yes, what can I do for you?", she asked. "Well, plenty, I guess," said Peter in his nicest smile. He briefed what he was doing in the company as a corporate planning strategist, how he got along very well with his boss, who had mentioned that he should be promoted in half-a-year's time, and wondered whether Arnold had been told about his situation.

"Oh, don't worry about this yet…Arnold is a very good assessor of people. He will reward people accordingly, if the person can read his mind, what he wants, expects, and pre-empts his thoughts and actions. I have worked for him for years now, and I do not have difficulties. Now let's talk about you…let's see you are married, and your wife is an equally successful executive at Xylec Inc. Hmm, how do I know? I make it my business to know, that's how I succeed", she smiled and crossed her long-legs. With her high heels, she must be at least 5' 11'', Peter thought. April then went into the background how she met Arnold, how she worked hard to understand Arnold and now they are a team. April advised that Arnold liked to have things done his way, as he has never been wrong so far. Arnold has taken risks that April has never seen before taken by other executives, and that's how Arnold became an achiever. "Let

Arnold have his say, do it, and if it doesn't work, then go back to Arnold, who will always have a solution" April suggested. "Shall we say the meeting with Arnold is not necessary, now?"
"Damn," Peter thought to himself, "how am I going to move up?"

5   The Professional Networker ~The Facts I

Tom met up with Paul after a number of tries on finding a mutually convenient time. Paul brought with him his diary...and that's all. Tom expected Paul to come up with loads of information and piles of printed stuff. After the initial exchange of pleasantries, Paul started the serious conversation.

"So, Paul, are you serious when you said you wanted to meet up with me to find out what I am doing? You know, I have been trying to meet up with you but you were always busy, with work, with Shirley...", Paul paused. "What made you change your priorities?" Tom related how the harder he worked, he never seemed to be able to keep up with the demands of bills and household expenses, now that he has a family. What was worse, he seemed to have less and less time to spend with Shirley and his daughter, Alison.

Hmm, Paul told him. This is the irony with working. Paul drew for Tom the figure below?

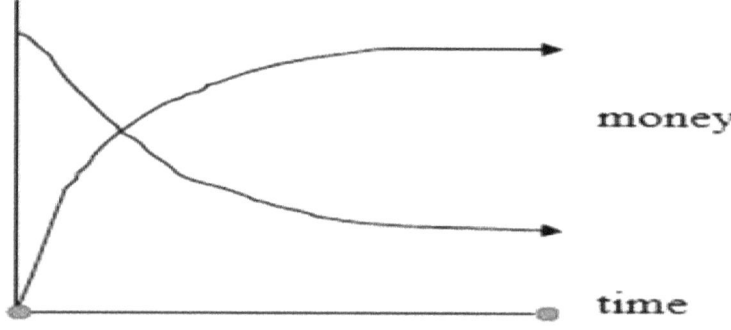

Paul told Tom that as he becomes more successful, he has less time, because he has to take on additional responsibilities. He may have more assistants to work under him, but that takes even more time because now he has to work through people. He has to train them, that takes even more time. "Do your boss stay late?", Paul asked. Tom nodded his head, and the more Tom thought about it, Tom realised his boss worked the latest, and seldom takes leave. That's not what I want...Tom mused. Yes, his boss rose rapidly in his position, but his boss also was more stressed.

When his boss's wife was expecting, his boss could only take 2 hours off to see his wife, and then he had to return to the company, which was rushing to meet its deadlines. There were always deadlines.

Tom shrugged his shoulder, "Maybe, that's what we are paid for, I guess?". I guess that is life, Tom accepted with resign. What can I do?

5   The Corporate Executive ~ The Facts I

Peter felt that he had to win the confidence of April, and then invite her to share her views how he could move up, now that Arnold has "installed" a gatekeeper to filter people wanting to see him as the new chief.

April seemed to be Arnold's right-hand person, and many of company's decisions seemed to be delegated more and more to her to act upon. Peter also noticed that Arnold seemed to spend an awful lot of time with her, discussing. Peter took up his courage and decided to have an appointment with April to discuss his issues after office hours. He would have preferred to have spent his time with Arnold so that he knows where he would be going in the company, or with Elizabeth, whom he was having less and less time now.

April was free on Wednesday evening, his squash day. Peter had no choice; he had to see April as soon as possible. "Thanks for coming, Peter," April gave her a nice smile. "No, thanks for making time available for me," Peter returned her smile. "Now what was it you wanted to discuss?". Peter told her about his promotion, and his future with the company. "Oh, don't worry. You are still young, we need you," she assured him. April looked no older than Peter, but already she was in charge, and Peter wished he was in the same position. "You know," she said, "we need to know who is on our side, and who is not. You need to be in the inner circle, if you need to move up," she pointed her finger upwards. "In this world, it is not what you know, but who you know, and who can move you up. Peter, if you are smart, you can be my assistant. Corporate Planning is only a small job. Be an executive assistant, and you can go far. You, me, Arnold, "she said in her husky voice. "But what about the promotion which my previous boss promised?", Tom enquired. "Ah, new boss, new rules...you know. Are you game, Peter?". Tom was a bit perplexed. What is involved? What is he expected to do? What new roles is he to undertake? He thought deep and hard. This means no promotion. He had to prove himself again to a new boss. His calls to his old boss to join him were not successful as his old boss was still trying to establish himself in his new position. Running a new subsidiary was a bit different from running the Corporate Planning Division.

Maybe he should try the new boss, who appears to be reasonable. "Yes, why not?", he answered, almost to himself. April seems to be a pleasant colleague and that is no reason why he should not succeed. One day, he will have to work with entirely new people, if he is to be CEO. "Good, ...do you know where we could have dinner and discuss your future?", April asked. Peter. He first called Elizabeth to apologise that he won't be back for dinner.

5   The Professional Networker ~The Facts II

Paul saw the expression on Tom's face. "Cheer up, man", there's more to it. "Have you heard about planning your time? Let me show you how:

How much time do you have?			
1 week = 7 days x 24 hours	= 168 hours		
work = 5 days x 8 hours	= 40 hours	balance =	128 hours
sleep = 7 days x 7 hours	= 49 hours	balance =	79 hours
eat = 7 days x 3 hours	= 21 hours	balance =	58 hours
others = 7 days x 4 hours	= 28 hours	balance =	30 hours
family =	20 hours	balance =	10 hours

All of us have 168 hours. When we utilise the hours for all the above activities, we have left 10 discretionary hours. Is that good? If you are more successful, you will be promoted, or given more responsibilities. The time for eating, family and for driving, leisure will be taken away, so that even the 10 discretionary hours will no longer be there. This is why spouses and children get less time than office. Work takes up more than three-quarters of your time. When you retire after a 40-40-40 plan, you then have more leisure time (i.e. the 128 hours), but then you have less income to be involved, and you are so much older, you pass many of the things you want to do. Is this what you want?"

"The 40-40-40 plan is to work 40 years, 40 hours a week and then retire with a $40 watch, which the company may give to you, but which you do not need anyway, after you retire."

"Or, you can use the 10 hours a day anyway to build up an asset upon which you may retire in 2 years, 5 years or even 10 years, instead of 40 years?"

"Retire in 2-5 years' time," Tom thought, that would be fun. "Alison would be 5 years' time. I would only be 35 and Shirley would be only 33. That would be fun."

But how? I only have 10 hours a week?

Paul saw Tom's face lit up and smiled...

5   The Corporate Executive ~ The Facts II

Peter drove April to his country club as April was quite new to the town. He requested for a private dining room so that he would not be disturbed during the discussion. Elizabeth as usual was working late as executive assistant to the Vice President of Xylec.

When Peter drove April to the club, there were many admiring glances at April who was not only tall but she was really good looking. When he was walking towards the dining room, he met some frequent club diners, who would wink and smile at him. Peter felt a bit annoyed. He was not having fun; he was trying to plan his future. After recommending some food to April and ordering for both of them, he started to talk business with April. "Hold on, Peter," April smiled. "You are too business like. Let's chat first".

Peter was amazed that for April, who is the same age as him, she was emotionally more intelligent * than he expected. He had learned through the grapevine, and which is not taught at business school *, that establishing a relationship helps overcome many business barriers. This was why so many vied for a place at Havard Business School, as the network and business relationships helped many to advance in their careers. He should have known. Get to know the person first, before working on anything, whether business, or not.

He found through the casual chat that April learned a lot about life from her mother, who was a very successful businesswoman, but who had to give up her business when she nearly was divorced by her husband who felt neglected and was less successful than her. She is now an active investor, and earns good money from her investments. April was taught that good grooming and clothes make one more presentable and more acceptable. At an early age, she was taught how to read cues from people, how to be diplomatic and good skills with people*. To help April, her mother had mentored her in her career and placed her in positions where she could learn about business. Her credentials established, she applied to work with Arnold, whom she describes as a pure gentleman, but who was firm, assertive, persuasive and fair.

She liked working with Arnold. She spent a lot of time discussing issues and solutions with Arnold, won his confidence, and now is able to proceed as the right-hand person.

"Hmm...what else can I learn from her", Tom wondered. "She is good".

5   The Professional Networker ~The Facts III

Paul told Tom that by going to work, he has traded time for money. Hence, he has to go to work. "What happens if you do not go to work?", Paul asked. "Ha...no money!", Tom laughed. "That's right. It's like you have to fetch water every day. Every day, by going to work, you are carrying your bucket. Now, what happens if you are sick?", Paul asked. "Obviously, you don't get paid! ...unless you are an executive, a monthly salaried worker. Right?" Tom retorted. "Wrong, some workers are paid monthly, but they are daily paid by the hour; these are accumulated, and you may get paid, sometimes in firms by the week, sometimes every fortnight, for most, monthly. But what happens if you have a long illness? And you are sick for more than 100 days?", Paul gave the scenario. "You don't get paid beyond your entitlement, isn't it?

"Hmm" Tom thought about it. "Paul's right, but what can I do? I have my family to support?". "Think about the singers you know...once their songs are recorded, and their songs are sold, what happens? They get paid, year after year, after year, after year." Paul added. "How would you like to have something like this that pays you year after year after year? It's like having a pipeline, that takes a long time to build, but once its ready, the water keeps flowing...you don't have to carry buckets, day after day, after day?"

"I have a job...my family has to be fed...my bills have to be paid...expenses need to be met. According to you, I have only 10 hours per week discretionary time. How can I build this...how much money do I need to invest?" Tom rattled off a number of questions. "Hold it, hold it." Paul answered. "Let me show you how."

Paul asked Tom whether he heard about "leveraging". This means Tom need not have 10 hours, but he could have 10,000 hours or more. What Tom needed was to be trained first how to do the business, then he gets trained how to be a leader, and finally he trains others to duplicate him. If Tom could spend 10 hours a week, and he could approach, select and train others to duplicate him, he could have 10,000 hours per week if he is able to have 1,000 people trained – not all directly by him – by him and his leaders under him.

It was like MacDonald. It is able to sell millions of hamburgers, not by having one store, but by having more than 20,000 stores worldwide. That is leveraging. No matter how Tom works, there is no way he can have more than 24 hours a day; even if he could work up to 24 hours a day, he will probably collapse after three days! "Wow. That is a powerful concept," Tom thought. But surely it takes some sacrifice?

5   The Corporate Executive ~ The Facts III

Peter was intrigued with April. Same age as him, and she is already so senior in the company.

April told Peter that an executive needs to get to the centre of the web and be in the inner temple with the CEO if he/she wants to succeed. Its like spider webs...those in the centre are unharmed by the spider, those at the sides are stuck to the web, and are moved or ousted.

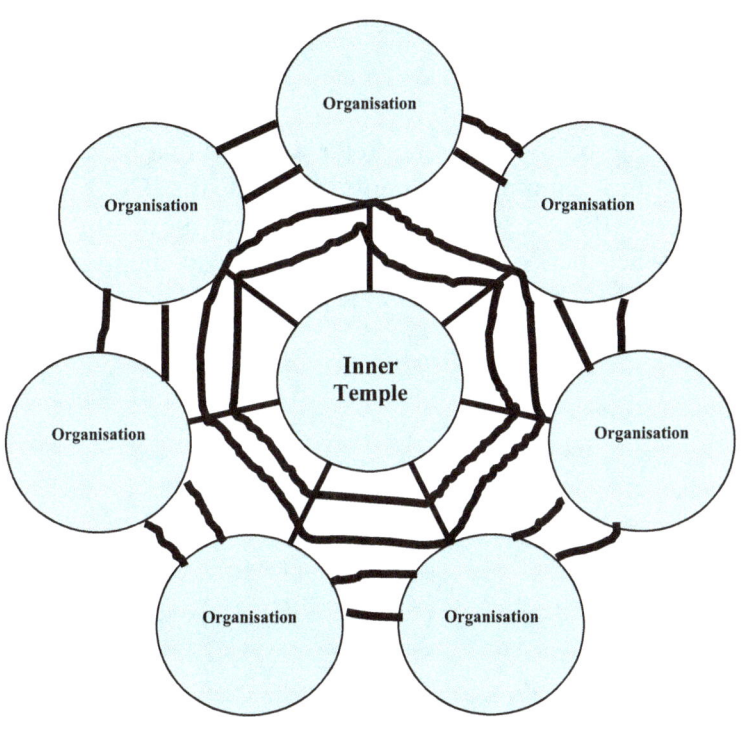

However, to be in the centre, Peter was told that he needs to spend a lot of time winning the confidence of the CEO or the senior executives. If successful, he becomes one of the senior managements. That's when perks and benefits are given to them generously, and compensation becomes very rewarding. However, this requires sacrifices.

6   The Professional Networker ~The Referral Network

Tom was concerned that he was already working very long hours. If he gets involved in this his time would even be worse. He would hardly then have time for Shirley and Alison.

"Look, you needn't worry," Paul said, as he saw Tom's forehead in furrows. "You have seen the movie, 'Titanic', haven't you?" Tom nodded. "After that, did you recommend to your friends? Did they go and see the film? Have your friends subsequently recommended to other people? And did you get anything from the cinema? Did the cinema give your money in return for your kind referral?" The answers were obvious to Tom. "This business is the same. It is called referral marketing. You use say a particular brand of toothpaste. You find it is good. What do you do? You recommend to your friend. Your friend recommends to others. And your referral grows. What do you get for this?" Tom answered, "Umbrellas?" "No," Paul laughed. "You get points for your friends purchase, your friends' friends' purchase. Then you get money in return. The more referral purchases, the bigger the points, the more money you get." "Hold it," Tom asked. "What is the catch?" Paul says, "There's no catch. You only need hard work. Remember your discretionary time? You need to use that on this referral."

"Won't your referral need to purchase a minimum amount? Won't I need to maintain a quota to get the money? Won't we all need to spend extra to get that extra?", Tom frowned. "What toothpaste do you use?", Tom asked. "Darlie". "What soap do you use?". "Lux". "What soap powder do you use?" This question-and-answer session went on. Paul told Tom that there is no additional purchase. Products supplied via the Internet by a company, which has catalogues from which one can buy all the said products, are substituting whatever is being bought for the household. By recommending them, one gets paid.

Paul also told Tom that all his family members, friends, work associates, suppliers to his household like the barber, newspaperman, the butcher, the lawyer, the banker, can all be part of his referral network. Once the network is large enough, Tom could get a steady stream of income, just like the pipeline Peter mentioned earlier.

Tom knew that between him and Shirley, they have a large network of contacts, but did not know that he could convert them into an income-producing asset for the family. That would be fantastic. However, how could he have the time?

6   The Corporate Executive ~ The Network

April next told Peter that to succeed he needs to have a network of close friends and associates, both inside the company and outside the company. CEOs and Board of Directors work on this basis. For instance, to borrow money from a bank, it is good to have formal channels, but having informal channels would shorten the paperwork. In business circles, timing is essential. Getting a verbal approval, and then working on the paperwork is different from working on the paperwork, then submitting for a bank loan. April told Peter how one phone call, to the CEO of a bank that she knew, for a $1 million loan which was approved within a few hours helped her credibility with her boss, who has since been very supportive of her whenever she wanted his endorsement of her decision. Hence, she spends a lot of time networking with people from all industries and at all senior levels.

Peter now knew why corporate executives work so late. They need to associate with people of influence and of power to help themselves to be influential and powerful. He recalls a friend, who happened to be a senior human resource executive, who would spend every evening after office hours to discuss with his boss, the CEO. Sometimes, it is just casual chat. That understanding and chemistry were important to be able to comprehend what the CEO wants.

Back at the office, Peter started to drop into departments that he would always be too busy to go to, and started to chat up executives, getting to know them. Previously, under his old boss, he was too busy number crunching for his boss, and would only be in contact with staff that he wanted materials, or vice versa. After work or during office, he started to call on associates that he knew only by phone, and started to have drinks and meals with them. He knew his network was important. To make sure that he had time for Elizabeth, he would sometimes ask her to join him in his networking activities. However, in serious business dealings, he had no choice but to leave Elizabeth out. There was less time now for Elizabeth now that he knew this was important for his career. He even suggested that Elizabeth start doing so for her climb up the career path.

Elizabeth started to have her own network of friends and associates that she wanted to cultivate that she could mutually call upon for help and assistance. However, with guys, sometimes she has to call Peter to be involved.

This networking was initially fun, but started to cost money and time.

7   The Professional Networker ~The Choice I

Tom was concerned that referral networking would take up so much time. Couldn't he instead start a business that would free him from employment so that he and Shirley would have more time together? Paul asked him, "Have you read 'Rich Dad, Poor Dad' by Robert Kiyosaki?". Paul explained to Tom why the choice of being a referral networker was the best choice:

E Employee	**B** Business
S Self-Employed	**I** Investor

Paul told Tom that the best quadrant is the I-quadrant, where one earns passive income, and it is akin to the pipeline concept. Money keeps flowing in whether one works or not. Most of us are in one of the three quadrants: employee (E) quadrant, self-employed (S) quadrant or in the business (B) quadrant. In these quadrants, we neither have time nor money, unless we have a large business with a system. Good examples are Microsoft or MacDonalds, where the owners have a system to duplicate and sell their products. Microsoft software, Windows operating system and Microsoft Word are duplicated around the world for sale, and every day, new users make the owners very rich. MacDonald's likewise with more than 20,000 franchises open a restaurant almost every one hour. They make their money for the owners through duplication.

While those in E and S quadrant have to work to earn their active income, those in the B quadrant make their active income faster by leveraging, and those in the I quadrant make their money passively, whether they are there or not, the money keeps flowing in because the money invested are in other businesses which generate profits to give them the passive income.

"So, Tom, your choice is to move from E quadrant to the B quadrant where you own a system to duplicate and leverage your time, and then be in the "I" quadrant to earn passive income." Tom thought about this.

7   The Corporate Executive ~ The Choice I

Peter had to work more than 10 hours a day in office and then network in the evenings. He found this taxing. When he meets up with Elizabeth for the night, both are too tired to talk and they drift off to sleep. They could only catch up during the weekends. How could he continue like this? He talked with April. April showed him his career path.

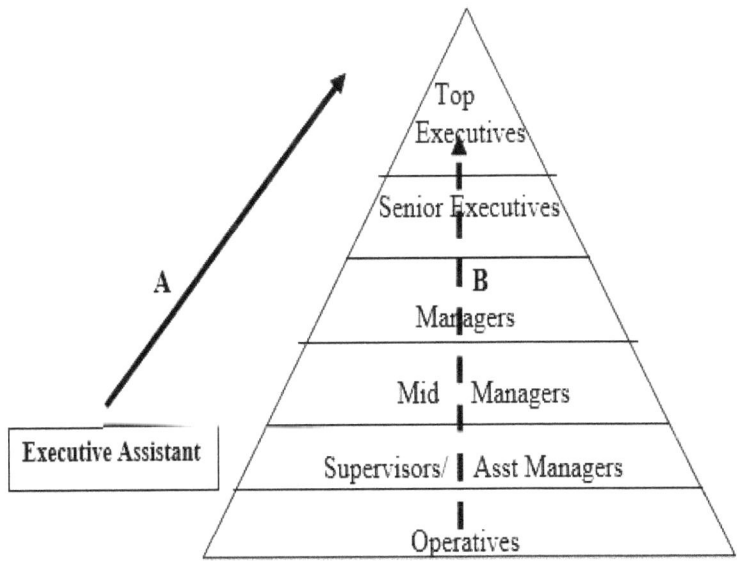

The path to the top is like a pyramid. Arnold is now the CEO, and he rose from rank and file. To fight to the top, you have to go through the hierarchy levels and you have to be noticed to move up faster. Arnold was the more daring of the rest and he could prove what he said he would do. He took risk and moved up. April told Peter that she chose the path B by working with the CEO as the executive assistant. By learning from the CEO, it is possible to know more about the business faster. Once she reaches senior executive level, she hoped that she could be given a department to run to prove herself to compete with the others. Despite her title as Executive Assistant, her ranking is mid-manager level. Peter as her Executive Assistant is now at supervisory level. Her plan is to move Peter up with a ranking of Assistant Manager level with a raise of salary to $65,000. So, while this is a staff function, with no direct line responsibility, the various departments that Tom has to deal with, and the fact that he works in the office of the CEO, will groom him to senior executive.

There was no guarantee that his career will be upwardly mobile, but the fact that the CEO will know him makes his career prospects bright. "Wow, a 30% rise in salary," Peter was delighted. But he knew he had to work his guts out. With that, he will get additional perks, like the key to the executive lounge and restroom. He knew he had made his choice.

7   The Professional Networker – The Choice II

Suddenly Tom realized what he has been in. For years, he has been schooled, educated and trained to be an employee. He knew some of his friends went on the self-employed career pathway. Equally, as both an employee or self-employed, there was little time and the money being made was not that lucrative that he and Shirley could have a good lifestyle: Flashes of what he envisioned came to him like lightning.

He should be enjoying his life with his beloved ones, Shirley and Alison, not spent time cooped up in the office with his colleagues and boss. Travelling and living in foreign countries for a prolonged period of time and savouring the culture was what he wanted for him and his family. Having a constant and growing income that goes into his bank account monthly would be what he was looking for. No cap on his earnings. Wow, not like his employment, where every year it was the same story ~ budget, achievement, ceiling on wage increase, and coming out of the performance appraisal with a sour taste in the mouth, regardless of his performance. Shopping with his spouse, no more arguing what to buy and how to buy (cash or credit). Alison can go to the finest schools without compromises. Living in a lovely mansion, with lots of greenery, overlooking a golf course and a lake. Waking up to beautiful sights and listening to the sounds of the sea waves, beating upon golden sands. Even if he were to leave the world, the duplication business Paul spoke about would take care of the financial needs of Shirley and Alison, as it was willable and sellable.

He also knew that this formula would give him both time and money, and not conflict one with the other, in traditional E and S earnings model.

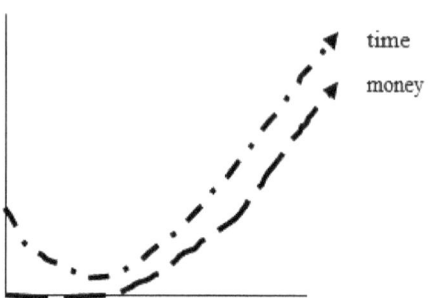

Tom also knew that initially, he would have less time and earn very little money, as Paul had told him that initially his (Paul's) pay check was about $8.90. But because he worked hard, Paul told him that he now earns five-figure income per month! Ironically, he now has more time.

7   The Corporate Executive ~ The Choice II

Peter thought about his new role in the inner temple of CEO's chosen and trusted group of follower-workers. Time was not his own now, as he has volunteered though April to trade his time for an upward career path and more money. He was excited.

He would be in the revered group that has access everywhere in the company. At times, he would be accompanying the CEO, initially with April, and then on his own, as trust and bond between boss and subordinate develops. He envisions travelling in the boss' stretched limousine and being accorded special privileges and attention whenever he goes to meetings. In due course, he will deputise for April as she moves up and he will represent the boss in meetings with the outside world. In international travel, because he would be representing the boss and the company, he would travel business class on jet planes and even first class, whenever the company's business warrants it. This means having access to hospitality lounges in airports, away from the rest of the economy class travellers. Company expenses will be his entitlement. If possible, he would take Elizabeth with him, if her presence does not deter the progress of the business. Wow, that will be fulfilling his dreams he had when he was in business school. In time to come, he would have a luxury company car if he does well. Already, April drives a medium range Mercedes, expenses fully borne by the company. He also understands that April had been given hefty bonuses since he worked as special assistant for the boss. That would give him and Elizabeth the opportunity to accumulate cash to buy an upmarket condominium that they always wanted, with swimming pool, jacuzzi and sports facilities. Club memberships would be part of the trappings of a successful corporate executive.

Peter was over the moon. Already he was given many files by April to look over and come up with proposals how the company should execute the plans. Despite the huge amount of paper, he has to pore over, study and work in details, he was very motivated to do his best. April would be his mentor. He has nothing to lose. The work involves tremendous amount of number crunching of "what-if" analyses and scenario planning.

He was excited. His MBA school has taught him a lot of this analytical and strategic stuff and he was ready to prove it in the real world.

8   The Professional Networker ~ A Talk with the Wife

Shirley waited for Tom as he sounded very excited of the business project he told her briefly over the phone. "What in the world has Tom got into this time?". Tom was always excited over projects, but would quickly cool down when he does not see the results.

Tom came home, with a very wide smile; he was very cheerful and kissed his wife and gave her a very warm embrace. Shirley responded happily, and received the bouquet of flowers Tom gave her. It's quite rare of Tom to do this. They had a quick dinner, had some wine and then sat in the lounge, with Tom explaining what Paul is doing.

"You mean Paul is making a good living, just talking to people about their dreams, networking with people and moving consumable products through his group?", Shirley asked. Assuring Tom that she was not being negative, maybe she did not have enough understanding how the networking business works, Shirley said, "You mean, after going through college, getting a degree, you are going into this project which does not need a formal education, and a paper qualification? What will people say?" Tom assured her that he was not going to quit his job, but that he needs to develop this project in the evenings, and when the income is large enough to replace his income from his full-time job, then he can quit his job and become a full-time networker. "How long will all this take? One year, two years? What about Alison? She is growing up and there is not enough time for both of us to bring her up. Have you thought about this?", Shirley put to Tom her concerns. Tom told her that he needs to invest time in order to get more time. Initially, he would need to take more of their spare time in the evenings to develop the business. To be able to be well off, Tom told her it would take 3-5 years. He would need her support. If the project worked, they will have a lifestyle they would never regret. If it did not work, Tom told her, they would not have lost anything. In fact, it would help Tom train to be an entrepreneur and be a better person, as his company is always encouraging intrapreneurship and leadership, skills he thought he would be better acquiring through this experience.

In addition, Tom said, he would need to invest a few thousand dollars, purchasing educational materials and attending seminars, to learn about the business, and work with mentors to develop the project to fruition. She would be a part of the project and he would take her to the meetings and seminars so she would also benefit from the association with networkers. Shirley told Tom she had reservations but to go ahead.

8   The Corporate Executive ~ A Talk with the Wife

Peter took Elizabeth to dinner in a fancy restaurant in town. They have always wanted to dine in this place but there was no opportunity or occasion until now. Peter arranged with Elizabeth so that she would also be able to make time for this dinner as she had a hectic schedule for the past few months, but she managed to persuade her boss that she need an early night off as she was working very late recently. She also needed the excuse to touch base with Peter. Peter had bought her a single rose and her favourite box of chocolates. He chauffeured her to the restaurant, gave his car to the car jockey and led her to the dining hall, which has one of the most beautiful chandeliers and decorations in town. After admiring the ambience of the environment, they settled down to have a conversation with a light drink and entre.

Peter told Elizabeth about April and her plans to draw him into the inner group of "inner temple" CEO's trusty executives. This would require dedication and intense work for specific periods and long hours. The payoff would be great, Peter explained. He might have to stay overnight in the office for days on stretch, but that would be learning and being groomed for upward career mobility. After explaining how their time together would be affected, he wanted her understanding and encouragement, so that both could be accommodating. Elizabeth apologised that she was also pretty busy herself, maybe both of them could meet each week for dinner or lunch. With that, Peter was pretty pleased that things would work out better than he expected.

"I hear that April is very attractive?" Elizabeth suddenly asked. Peter had never expected this as he looked at Elizabeth as a very efficient colleague, and who happened to be very good looking. Peter asked how did she know when both of them had never met? "Ah, this is a small business community. Both of us work in the same city. People see, observe and know who's who," Elizabeth smiled. Peter was surprised word has got round. "And April is also the number 2 person in the company. Of course, she gets noticed, especially if she is not only pretty but also capable, not like your Elizabeth.", she teased Peter. He loved Elizabeth, her sense of humour was what attracted her to him.

She knew Elizabeth was as capable as April, although the latter's beauty was known in the office. "Not to worry, she's my colleague and my immediate superior," Peter assured her. "Now, what do you think of the time and sacrifice required of both of us?", Peter asked. Elizabeth reminded Peter that their relationship was most important. "We must make time for each other".

9 The Professional Networker ~ How Does it Work?

Tom could not wait for Paul to show up since he has made a commitment to Shirley that he must ensure the family is not neglected while building up a network in the evening to build a pipeline of income and work in the day to earn the active income.

Paul chatted with Tom and then went into deep serious discussion. As Paul talked, Tom was advised to take down notes otherwise he would not be able to remember the key activities:

- Dream ~Paul told Tom to start thinking about his dream, which meant that Tom needs to discuss with his spouse why he needs the business badly. "You need the dream to help you when you are down, especially when you find obstacles impeding the progress of your plans". Tom was also asked to state 100 things he would like to do if time and money were not constraints.
- List~ Paul told Tom to list down all the relatives and close friends he had, then work on the business associates he knew and finally include people whose names he had but were not so familiar. The last was people he noticed but who were total strangers. He was told not to pre-judge them.
- Invite Them~ While we are very familiar with inviting friends and business associates for social events or business events, Tom was told he need to learn how to invite people properly and professionally for this business.
- Show them the Concept~ On a piece of paper, show the friends, associates or invitees, the concept of referral network building. Go through the numbers. Most would not understand it for the first time but the numbers are important to interest people. There would be three outcomes: some will join to buy products; others may join to build a small business and those who will not

-
-
- respond as the business concept is not comfortable to them for one reason or another.
- Products~ Recommend products you have used to the friends, associates or even strangers. They will find one or more products that they will need. With a large group of people, the total turnover will be huge.
- Personal Development~ As this business needs continuous motivation and training, Paul told Tom to read books, listen to tapes on how others became successful and learn their techniques, attend meetings.

Tom was surprised the steps were so simple.

9   The Corporate Executive ~How Does It Work?

April was told by Peter how much she is known in town, that his wife Elizabeth even knew about her. April was flattered, but Peter did not elaborate further. Well, now that the commitment was made, April laid down some ground rules for Peter to follow, and requested that perhaps, Peter should jot down the points:

- Know the CEO~ it was important to know the leadership and management style of the CEO. No two CEOs are the same. Arnold was a boss who likes to delegate without abdication. Arnold also expects a lot of backing from his subordinate, who is expected to know in details all transactions of the matter being discussed at hand. The subordinate must know when to speak up and when to allow the CEO to carry on, even sometimes making public statements and decisions that would contradict what the subordinate has planned in the proposal. One way to avoid this is to meet with the CEO regularly and read his mind, understand and learn how to pre-empt his decisions. Checking back with the CEO was an art, without being too upfront with it. If the CEO changes, he must be prepared to change.
- Be Prepared and Attend to Details ~ as the CEO was always skimming through details and focusing only on key essentials, his assistant must be very thorough in his work and research to come up with a plan or proposal. If the document is not well prepared and there are glaring mistakes, always ensure that there is room for correction. Never be stubborn, unless you are very, very sure.
- Use Numbers to Persuade, and Opinions to Sway~ No proposal can stand cross-examination without sufficient number crunching. Inputs from Opinion Leaders can help the decisions to be made.
-

- Work in the Background ~ To move a proposal, make sure there is sufficient background work is done to influence stakeholders inside and outside the company. This is not easy, especially in matters where discretion is

- Be Discreet~ "you will never know what is sensitive when you work for the CEO's office", April advised. Therefore, do not bring up the matter or even the code name unless the CEO has brought it up or the subject has been exposed to certain individuals. Money issues and sensitive political & personal matters are examples.

- Always be Available~ Always be contactable, as there would be urgent information or documents that need to be retrieved. Hence, the CEO has issued personal handphones for senior executives and his close aides. This means he/she is always on call, even during vacation.

10   The Professional Networker ~ The Dream

Paul told Tom he will help Tom to visualize his dream. The dream is being able to do all the things Tom desired that he thought was impossible. Unrealized dreams are due to the state of mind and environment conditioning which makes one to compromise. How many people have said, "I'll take it easy, let the day come by." when they thought they could not achieve their dreams. Paul told Tom how some people have realized their dreams:

- Getting the car he always wanted ~ there was a networker who used to work in the lowly job of repairing dents and bumps on the bodyworks of cars. However, he always dreamed how he could own one of the luxury sports cars, as he always was working to repair cars but could not dare dream of it. Because his sponsor told him he could achieve anything he wanted if he worked on it, he would always visualize the car he wanted, the colour, the smell of the leather and even the model of the car. Many years later, this ambitious man not only was able to buy a BMW 2-seater sports car, he also later changed to a silver Porsche!
- Savings of $100,000 in the bank ~ another networker dreamed of the day when he had a spare amount of $100,000 in the bank. He wanted to achieve this because he never had much money left for him and his family. Although a profession as an engineer sounded grand, he or his could not afford to buy any items that was above average. His wife would window shop for ages and then compromise on a pair of shoes, which was on sale. He worked furiously to build his network, and now not only he had more than $100,000 in his bank; he and his wife went shopping at the last minute before their trip overseas and spent over $25,000 in less than one hour. They could afford it.

- Charity ~ as a youth, he and his friends would skip lunch by sitting in the school dining room to symbolise that they would help the hungry of the world by not eating any noon meal that day. Later in his exposure to the real world, he realized that empty plates do not feed the poor.

- When he became a successful networker, he founded a foundation, Mercy Corps, which not only raised millions, they could give medicine, supplies and food for the impoverished in Afghanistan and Africa.

- Scholarships~ a university professor of music was not always well off, when she had to feed her young children single handedly. Now, she has raised an international network that could give music scholarships every year to talented students and started a children hospital in India for the children.

10   The Corporate Executive ~ The Dream

Peter was given a heft raise in his new role as executive assistant to April and to the President. He was given corporate expenses and credit cards for his use and for official duties. When necessary, he could call upon the company's limousine to take him to meetings and pick him up conveniently. The parties meeting up with him was always impressed with the young man who was so well provided, unlike many young executives who had to part far away and then walk to the meeting place. Peter wined and dined at company expenses without anyone questioning him.

This was the dream environment he always wanted. He also had power. Since he worked with the right-hand person of the CEO, he was conferred authority, respect and power. Whenever, he wanted information, effort was made to gather the information he wanted. He called for statistics on the last ten years of sales, manufacturing, costs, manpower, overheads, technical and sometimes, company-secret documents, and these would be delivered to him as soon as they were available. Not all the information was readily in the form he wanted, and that was why his role called for. He could also call upon any of the senior executives and junior staff to assist and they would be very willing and cooperative. Although there were some envies among the older staff, Peter knew because of his qualifications, although he lacked experience, he could count on them to work as a team.

The company called upon Peter to re-craft the vision and mission of the company, which the CEO felt was not encompassing enough to reflect the changes of the environment. As the company was in manufacturing and sales, Xylec's vision and mission was to "supply services and products in computer network, communications and electronics at the best superior service by topping all competition". In reality, the company was about the fifth in the industry and had market share of only 18%. Everyone knew the reason why Xylec lost market share as it did not include the internet technology and its network & communications technology was obsolete. By calling for the company's feedback, and holding a visioning workshop so that everyone could recast the vision and mission.

Peter found that within two weeks, he had the new vision and mission ready, since the cooperation from everyone was so readily available.

The new vision and mission were "Our firm believes in state-of-the-art technology to deliver network, communications, electronics and internet services and products to the satisfaction of our clients by superior employees' teamwork". This initial success made Peter believe in his "dream" job!

11   The Professional Networker ~ 100 Goals

Tom sat down with Shirley to work out his Dreams and then followed by 100 things both of them wanted individually and together. What was it that they wanted badly that they were willing to work hard and late into the night. They started to work out their Dreams:

> "Our dream is to be able to have generous amount of quantity and quality time together so that we can spend time travelling, enjoying the world, inculcating good values, educating and learning, with our children.

We believe in God and wish to dedicate our time to worship God, and it si our dream to travel to all those places sacred and holy to our God, so that we can revere and understand his creations.

For this we need time, money, family bonds, good interpersonal skills and human values. We need the financial freedom in 5 years' time, by the year 2xxx. "

Tom and Shirley knew that this was their first draft of their dreams. Now they need to be more specific in writing down their goals:

- To be good parents to Alison, and all the other children we will bear~ be more patient with Alison, to spend more time listening to her, and talking to her.
- To travel to the following countries and cities, not on a package tour, but to stay at least two weeks, to savour the culture and to understand the lifestyle of each country: -
    - France, Paris
    - Italy, Rome
    - Switzerland, Geneva

- Britain, London, and Wales
- Scandinavian countries, Oslo
- Russia, Moscow
- U.S., Hawaii, Colorado Rockies, New York, Boston town and universities, San Diego, San Francisco
- Japan, Tokyo

- Australia, Sydney
- China, Shanghai and Beijing
- South Africa, Johannesburg
- Pacific Islands: Palau, Marianas Islands
* To visit Holy Places: Jerusalem

Tom knew he would take some time to complete this but this has started.

11   The Corporate Executive ~ Goals

Peter knew that he needed to set his corporate goals every year, what he wants to accomplish in relation to his work and how the goals get higher and higher. He learned this, working with his previous boss. Based on this, he would be appraised and then there is the annual negotiations with his superior. He was disappointed that despite his good performance, he found his boss was promoted and his move to the next step of the corporate ladder was interrupted. He hopes this will not have to repeat itself as April had already told him that if the CEO changes, he will have to manage the change. He wished he could be in more control. Already there were 5 performance measures that he must meet.

Peter wrote his goals:
- Achievement: To deliver all proposals and output documents on time and on demand to the CEO's office.
  He put down that where it was beyond his control, he would not be able to produce the proposal and plan on time. However, he knew it was not acceptable to the administration. Sometimes, the information is not available in the company and he has to use commercial intelligence and his network to secure the data. This was what he was paid for. He was very uncomfortable with this. He also wrote down that he hoped not to be disappointed with the promise given by the last boss.
- Teamwork: To work with all the team members for strategy, plan formulation, and implementation to achieve corporate goals, i.e. for year 2xxx, achieve a sales and profit target of $450 million and $45 million respectively.
  Peter was not uncomfortable working with all the senior executives and the executives across the board. However, achieving the sales and profit targets were something else, as he

was not directly responsible for bottom-line results, although his papers would be instrumental in directing the company initiatives, with inputs from everyone.
- Development: To develop his skills and knowledge in financial management and develop a team to support the tasks in the company.
  This was not an issue for him.

- Public Service: To serve in the Community Club and undertake 5 activities.
  He loved this kind of work. Time was however an issue.
- Advancement: To move up the career path to be senior executive assistant.
  Peter knew this was not easy as April is the vice president.

One thing he noted; none of these dealt with his own and family goals.

12   The Professional Networker ~ List

Tom was told by Paul to write down all the people he would like to show the plan to. As Tom and Shirley are quite private people, Tom thought how would he be able to come up with 100 names. However, he knew that if he was serious about this business, and his bread-and-butter depended on this, he put his mind into creating the list.

He started with all his relatives and Shirley's relatives: he had 7 brothers and 4 sisters. Together with Shirley's 5 siblings, and their children, some of whom have grown up and have their own families, he could easily put down at least 20 names. From a recall of his close friends and Shirley's close friends, that would generate at least 10 names. Then he started to think of people outside his circle of contacts. His neighbours that he was familiar with would be about 5. His work mates would be about 7. Shirley's could put down 10 names. If he wrote down all those people he had contacted via his business firms, he could add another 20 that he could comfortably deal with. That's when he got stuck. Who else could he call on? Try as he and Shirley could, he could only think of another 5 names. That was 77 names. With that, he anxiously waited for Paul to meet up with him the next day.

Paul smiled at him and congratulated him. He told Tom he did a very good job at producing 77 names! Not many could produce such a long list. Tom felt good. Paul was very good at encouraging him and Shirley. They could call on Paul and he would always be there at hand to advise and help. "What about your lawyer? your banker? your butcher? your newspaper man? your plumber? your electrician? your car mechanic? your church elders? your favourite restaurant owner?" Paul asked. Tom got the idea. Anyone he came contact into regularly. From each person, at least 3 referrals, and he would have his 100 names in no time!

Before he knew it, Tom had listed over 120 names.

Paul then asked Tom to go through the list and describe the people in the list. Are they married? How many kids? What was their profession? What do they like to do in their spare time? Do they like travelling? Sports? Are they respected in the

community?

By going through the list, Paul told Tom he could pick out those who were singles or couples, respected, ambitious, professionals and frustrated with their positions and wanted to change. That led to a group of about 25 names that Tom could focus on as the first priority to contact and show them the concept.

12   The Corporate Executive ~ List

Peter was given a diary since he started work as a corporate executive, and he has developed a habit of putting down the list of things he had to do. Most of it were dates for meetings, and sometimes he has to juggle the dates to ensure that he is able to accommodate all the meetings. Initially, he would pen down all appointments. But he learned through his boss that sometimes he has to decide:

- the urgent and important   (I)
- the urgent but not important   (II)
- the not-so-urgent but important   (III)
- the not urgent and not important. (IV)

Category I items are those that will affect the company and his future. For instance, for a mergers and acquisition meeting, he has to provide the analyses with several scenarios for the business conditions. The paper must be in at all costs, and the timing must be met. He must deliver the proposal, there is no negotiation, on time and on budget. Category II are those items that he must attend to, otherwise it may cause more problems later on. Getting the staff to agree to an early meeting so that he can come out with the paper. He needs to inform the personally on the exact data requirements. He has time for this so that he can adjust when the data is due, as sometimes the data is not available in-house. Sometimes, his personal matters come into this list, like calling Elizabeth that he could not meet up with her. That call is most urgent, but sometimes he could not get through to her, and he will send SMS message through to her handphone. Category III items are not urgent, and these are sending to the staff the format of the report required. Although not urgent, it is important, since if the data comes in a non-uniform format, he will spend an awfully long time to convert those data. As he need time to come out with the format, sometimes he would tell the staff he needs the information and then send the format in an e-mail. Category IV items are those items that he could drop, such as lunch or dinner appointments with friends and colleagues, for social and acquaintance reasons. Or meetings that needed input from him, as a member of the company's employee. His presence or absence would not impact the company, and he would decline these appointments.

Peter's problems arise when he has a list of matters to attend to and he is not sure if that needs attention immediately. He was caught on a couple of occasions when he thought the matter was important but not urgent when he found his former boss asking for the report. He had to stay overnight to produce the report. Now, he had developed his judgement when to decline, accept, postpone or urgently work on assignments.

13 The Professional Networker ~ Invitations

Tom was never taught formally or informally how to invite contacts to show them the networking business concept, although in work, he has developed his own style of inviting business colleagues. Because of his position, his invitation to people outside or inside the company was quite easy. However, getting free information was not so easy. In this networking business, Tom was taught by Paul that inviting people to talk about the networking business was not that easy, but if done professionally, would interest most individuals. He took down the advice given by Paul. The principles were:
- never talk about the business over the phone. Make an appointment.
- always be brief.
- ask questions, listen and don't make statements.
- set two dates for the appointment. If not free, then call to make appointment another time.
- say, "are you open to suggestions to be financially and time free?", or "I am involved in a business project and I am looking for key people to join me in this venture. Will you be interested?"
- once appointment has been made, confirm the time, place and venue, and hang up.

If invitation is made in person, the same principles apply. The prospect may ask," what is it about?", or "is it direct sale?", Paul warned. "Just say that, 'I can't talk now as I have to be brief, but I have to run through some numbers with you. It is more than direct sale (if this is asked)".

Paul also cautioned Tom that the meeting should never take place in the office as it would not be an ideal venue for such a serious discussion. Preferably, it should be at the prospect's house, together with the prospect's spouse. If not, meet at a quiet restaurant or in a quiet place in the mall.

If the prospect is ready, then Tom should there and then ask the prospect to give the names on the list a call straight away, then pass the phone to Tom to speak to the prospect's friend or associate to confirm that, and make an appointment there and then.

Tom was relieved that he had someone like Paul to show him the shortcuts and get into settings that works.

13   The Corporate Executive ~ Invitations

Although Peter was inundated with work, sometimes he would get an invitation to attend functions organised by investment bankers, companies, consultants or seminar management firms. He used to attend them, until he had so much work piling up. April then called him and mentioned that she has not seen him in these functions. She wanted to introduce him to her business associates. Peter smiled and apologetically told her that he was snowed under with work. April advised him that he should put aside time for such functions, since he need to be in touch with the business community. The contacts will come in handy for his work and for moving up in the City. Hard work will help but getting roped into the business network was equally important.

With that advice, Peter would work, then rush to functions, meet the people, make some excuse and return to his desks. At times, there would be more than 3 invitations for cocktail and buffet in a week. Though stretched for time, he tried to make it. And April, no matter how busy, was always at these functions with her boss, Arnold, who would attend only functions that he thinks that are strategically important both for him and the firm.

As he made his rounds of the cocktail parties, he found that he was meeting regular business people, who eventually became his acquaintances, from whom he could generate mutual interests. From there, some became his friends that he would gather together with Elizabeth when they have their own private social gatherings. He found that they were similarly inundated with work but had to attend such social functions to develop their own circle of business contacts. Quite a number of such regular attendees became their customers and clients, and many became their sources of information to further their work.

Soon, Peter began to enjoy the break from work by attending these functions. However, it meant that he had to work even later in the office, and his time spent together with Elizabeth, was limited to weekends. Peter found that he spent more time with April in the office than with Elizabeth, his future partner in life.

That was a paradox. However, he was glad that April was there as a mentor.

14   The Professional Networker ~ Show the Plan (I)

Paul and Tom would meet regularly to discuss the business. Tom made an appointment in the presence of Paul and managed to secure an appointment with a friend, Solomon. The appointment was on Tuesday night the following week at 8p.m. in his friend's house, about 5 kilometres away. After the first successful appointment, Tom was told that there would be three outcomes: the prospect would be just a customer, just buying products, a small business builder, hoping to build a small income part-time, or a network builder, someone who would work very hard to be financially free. He told Tom to be prepared.

Tuesday night came. Tom was very anxious and he has told Shirley all week about this appointment. He had not been so excited before. He was never that excited about his work. This was different.

Paul and Tom arrived at Solomon's house in Paul's car, as they had earlier made a rendezvous at a shopping mall where Tom would park his car. As they drove there, Tom briefed Paul about the prospect. Solomon was his classmate in high school. He was not a leader in the class but was very quiet in class, worked diligently, and had his close circle of friends. He now works as an accountant, being the more studious of his class. Tom said he did not know Solomon's wife and has not met her.

Solomon opened the door, and Tom hugged him as they have not seen each other since high school. Tom introduced Paul to Solomon as his mentor and as a very successful business entrepreneur. Together they would show him the business. Solomon called his wife, Angie, who was a very petite lady, who seemed familiar to Tom. He found out that she was from the same high school but a year junior to them. After the initial introductions and catching up on some old times, Paul started asking Solomon and Angie what they did on weekends and on vacation. They spent their time working part-time so that they could build their dream home. They had been doing this for as long as they have graduated from college. Their plan was to work as much as they could in their early years and then retire by the age of 45. They then plan to travel round the world. So far, they are about one-third of their goal.

Paul asked them if he could show them the option that they could realise their dreams much earlier, would they be interested? Instead of them working part-time to earn extra income, would it not be faster if they could leverage their time and have a group of persons who could duplicate them? Solomon and Angie could be trained so that they can show others how to do the business as well. Would they be interested? That night, Tom got his first downline.

15   The Corporate Executive ~Doing the Work

Peter was told by April on Monday that their firm, Xylec, would be taking over Com-Com and they need to "camp-in" for the next three weeks while negotiations are underway. Arnold has already commenced discussions with the owners, two brothers, Mike and Harry Williams, and there was a break-through during the meeting on Sunday night. Com-Com build network for companies that run internet businesses, using Linux, the open-source operating software. This means that the cost of purchasing the company would be lower than if the company used proprietary software like Microsoft, Oracle or SAP. Peter must work with April and their team to figure out what would be the right figure to propose to their CEO, during this period when they would be carry out "due diligence" assessment of Com-Com. In addition, they have to line up all the financing for the deal. Arnold deals in round numbers, and April has to figure out how it should be done. Com-Com has sales of $150million, $250 million and $ $400 million for the past three years respectively, and earnings before interest and depreciation of $20million, $25million and $32million. The usual multiplier for such acquisitions would be no more than 5 times the net profit; however, where the acquisition is more strategic, where there is strategic fit of the business, the premium paid can be higher, so that even 10 to 20 times.

Peter had a problem. He had been neglecting Elizabeth, and now this has cropped up. He immediately called her, explained what is happening and gave a sigh when Elizabeth said, "I understand". Next, he almost ran to the conference room where about 10 staff, mostly young executives from the accounts department, and one senior vice president for corporate development had already gathered. April briefed them of their mission, timing, the task and secrecy of the deal. "Nothing must leak from this room", she cautioned. They pored over the materials as Elizabeth went over the company profile, what data they had available and what they lacked. Work started. Peter set up the financial spreadsheet using Excel software that he was so adept. Com-Com had given their financial spreadsheet in diskettes. When he tried to load the data, he found problems. Theirs was in Lotus format. When Peter tried to convert them into Excel format, there were many significant errors. Peter had to rush to April to find the contact in Com-Com so that he could

liaise with them.

April told Peter there must be no contact, as they did not want to alert them that they were seriously considering their offer of sale. Peter shook his head. He rushed over to the IT department to find out if they had Lotus software. The IT department was puzzled as all their company software was of one format. Peter could not explain the reasons…!

14   The Professional Networker ~ Show the Plan II

Tom was over the moon. So quickly, he thought. And I need only six persons and I am free! He has already one prospect who has signed up. How this is his first downline. Paul briefed Tom as they were leaving Solomon's house that Tom must maintain the relationship with Solomon and Angie by regularly encouraging them to attend the network meetings and show the plan to others. This also means that Tom must know quickly learn how to show the plan! He must also learn how the counsel his downline. As Paul talked, Tom's mind was racing with all kinds of thoughts. So much to learn in so short a time. At the end of the journey as Paul dropped Tom off to pick up his car, Paul told him, "Don't worry, I will help you". That was very reassuring. "Keep calling and making appointments".

Tom excitedly told Shirley of his experience in signing up Solomon and Angie. Shirley congratulated Tom. No, Tom told her, the congratulation was for both as they made a decision to build the business. That night, both Tom and Shirley could not sleep well, as they felt that they would be free by Saturday, if he were to sponsor one person a night.

Next day, Tom called up 10 persons for an appointment. Most of them could not make it as they had something on, or was too busy, and quite a few said they were not looking for something to do as they had kids and their job was taking too much of their time to spare. Tom conferred with Paul. The first thing Paul asked was "did you ask them questions?". Oops, that was the first mistake. Tom was so excited he kept on talking that he forgot the first basic principle. Okay try again. Tom called number 11. "If time and money were right, could we meet to discuss a business project I am involved in?" Number 11 was Henry, who is now self-employed, running a supermarket. He would be free, but only after 10 in the night when he closed up. Tom agreed on the time and place and met Henry on Wednesday, two days later. Henry was looking for such a business that will give him more time. As a self-employed, he is in control of his work but he has little time as his small supermarket store was long hours. He signed up as a network distributor. Then he said he has no time to attend the meetings. "I will come back to you on this", Tom promised.

Paul knew about such persons having no time for meetings. He told Tom to pass to Henry a tape on time and money. That will convince him that he needs to invest his time if he wants to have time.

15   The Corporate Executive ~ Doing the Work II

Peter cannot divulge the reasons for needing Lotus software. Although Excel software can read data in lotus, doing so makes the format run all over the place and Peter would have to go through each line and rectify the errors. Hmm. I need special permission to purchase the Lotus software. He checked with April: "...spend the money first and then claim it back as merger & acquisition activities expenses". That was quick and what a solution. Peter drove his car to the local software store in town, picked up the right version of the software and raced back to the office. He loaded the software on his computer and started converting the file into Excel form. To make sure that data was correctly converted, he printed the files from the Lotus format first. That was a mistake. It took almost three hours, as the spreadsheet was huge and after printing it, he had to paste them together, then shrink it via photocopying. By the time he got the spreadsheet in Excel in his computer, four hours had passed by. Meanwhile, the other 11 officers of the company were waiting for his spreadsheet to be setup, and seeing the delay, had manually extracted key data from the reports that were available at hand.

Peter did quickly some financial ratios and trend analysis. As they analysed the graphs, they realised that the net earnings margin was falling rapidly although sales and earnings increased over the past three years. Some expenses were eating away the profits. They needed to check on these. The team pored through the reports including analysts' reports on Com-Com. Nothing gave a clue, although depreciation showed a rise. Peter requested a meeting with the owners of the company to understand the financial figures. April told him she has already put in the request through Arnold. Wow…April is fast; she already sensed something needed clarifying. Next evening when most of the staff had gone back, Peter and April and a team of analysts from Xylec visited the Com-Com. They met with the owners and were given a tour of the plant. Most of the machines were not operating as it was after 7p.m. and the plant stopped work after 5p.m. One line was still operating as they were rushing some orders. As they toured the plant, Peter and April noticed in one of the sections, there were large number of stocks in the store unshipped. Peter asked one of the workers why the stocks was in the store. "Oh, these are obsolete.

After returning from customers, these became unshippable," he said innocently. There and then, both knew they had the answers. The company shipped large amounts of goods to distributors which returned them. Peter knew that he had to make adjustments to the stocks and that would reduce the price Xylec had to pay Com-Com. No more than 5 times the earnings.

16 The Professional Networker ~ How Money is Made

Paul showed Tom that money is made as shown in the diagram:

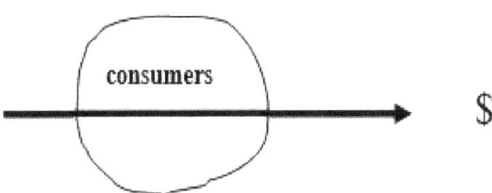

As products are bought and consumed by the public or the distributors, money is made. A large network will result in a larger amount of money. Hence, there must be a balance between retailing products for consumption by the public and distributors, and creating a network. The larger the network, the larger the consumption, and the larger the money. It is similar to wholesalers and retailers who earn from the wholesalers and retailers' margins as products are wholesale or retailed through these intermediaries.

To enable the public and distributors in using the products, the networker must first use the products so that he/she can know the properties, features and benefits of the products. Hence, the networker can then recommend the products for use by those in his group.

To start off, Tom started to check the brochure and the online catalogue for the products that he could purchase, especially those that he could substitute. It made no sense for Tom to purchase from Walmart or the local pharmacist if he has already a business that he could buy from. A person who runs a Shell gas station would buy from his own gas station rather than from another neighbourhood station. Tom had no problem with this concept. For this to work, he first had to make sure he made financial arrangements with his bank so that there will be direct debit from his bank and any bonus, due to him as products from his group is being purchased, will be directly credited to him.

He also noted that any purchase from members introduced to the internet shopping directly or indirectly to him would also be counted as his group. This makes sense therefore for him to train his members he recruited how to further recruit their friends, associates and customers, so that they could duplicate him.

If Tom buys $200, his group purchase is $1,200.

Tom ⟶ A ⟶ A2 ⟶ A3
total=$1200 $250 $350 $400

16   The Corporate Executive ~ How Money is Made

Peter knows that Com-Com could be purchased for about $150 million cash. If Xylec was a listed stock, the purchase could be a mixture of cash and stocks, ranging from half cash to about 70% cash, depending on the negotiations. To purchase this in cash, means Xylec needs to raise $150 million from the financial institutions. Add in financing costs, the total purchase price could reach $200 million.

There were two ways Xylec could make money from this transaction: after taking over Com-Com, look at synergies between Xylec and Com-Com, and start trimming redundant staff, physical space, equipment and use common distribution, marketing and administration facilities. That could save the company about $15 to $20 million. Com-Com has other physical assets and equipment it sold that may not be in line with Xylec's core businesses. Hiving off these assets and equipment could bring in another $4 million. If sales could be increased by another $50 million after the merger, the net earnings could bring in another $5 million. That would result in a net purchase price of $174 million. How could he justify paying $174 million to bring in sales worth $450 million and net earnings of $37 million, assuming another $50 million could be squeezed from the purchase? This was making Peter stretch for ideas. One idea being floated by the team was that Com-Com should be run separate company, bring up its sales and profits to more than double, then list it. That would make Com-Com a billion-dollar company wholly owned by Xylec. If a 30% stake in Com-Com is then sold, Xylec would make $300 million to retire off the loan and then have the balance as cash reserves. Peter wonder if this would work?

The only issue here is that the market for taking the firm public may change and scuttle their plans. The takeover may raise the profile for

Xylec, and which if later listed after Com-Com, every employee would also benefit from the stock options. There were so many unknowns. So many "ifs". The team discussed the options, the problems and the solutions. Peter started to work on several scenarios, and came up with the financial outcome for each scenario. Finally, with the draft spreadsheets ready, they met up with Arnold, who was quickly briefed by April.

Arnold looked at the spreadsheets and the scenarios, he discussed with April, thought over for a while, then announced: "Okay, we will offer them $100 million, retain the management but we will have the right to re-shape and re-size the company, improve its sales and profits and then sell it for at least $ 500 million after 3 years, that's $130 million a year. How about that? let's go" The takeover was on.

17   The Professional Networker ~ Personal Development

Tom had to listen to Paul who advocated that he takes a personal development program in order to build the network properly. There were already successful networkers who are already millionaires and they have their experiences recorded on tapes. There were tapes on success stories by these entrepreneurs, tapes on techniques how to build the network and tapes on leadership. The most important was to listen to as many audio tapes as possible so that Tom can be mentally tough. Unlike his corporate job where Tom was used to deal in tens of millions of dollars, he has to prepare his mindset to descend to the lowest level and build up his foundation:

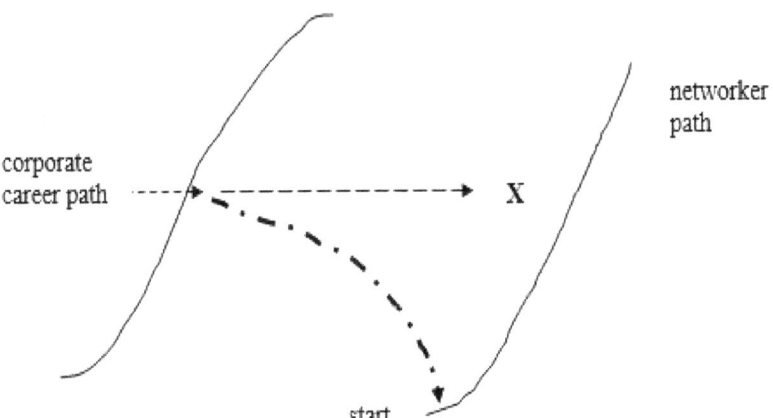

To prepare for this, Tom was to read books, like "The Magic of Thinking Big", "Positive Thinking" and "Parable of a Pipeline". This is because Tom had to build a foundation so that his income would be a continuous flow and he would not have to " keep fetching a pail of water" which is his analogy of going to work daily and not being paid if he is absent from work. In addition, Tom was told to prepare to attend the series of meetings which he had to bring people to, weekly, and monthly, and finally quarterly. Tom boggled at this. He had not been prepared of the extent of the networking. "This will take a life-time," Tom protested. Paul put his hands on Toms shoulder, "remember, Tom, you are building your own business under mentorship. You are not building MY business; you are building your OWN business. You need to be tough mentally. This is a change, but the rewards are enormous".

Tom's mind quickly turned to dream where he wanted to be his own boss, and not be on the 40-40-40 workplan, where after working 40 years, he gets a $40 watch and live on 40% of his last drawn salary in retirement. He wanted to give Shirley and Alison the comfortable life style he promised. It is not easy to transition to be a successful entrepreneur, but there are many successful people, and he wanted to be one of them badly.

17   The Corporate Executive ~Personal Development

Although Peter had worked hours and days on the financial scenarios, the quick decision by Arnold stunned him. That was done in less than half an hour, and he had given the strategy and the direction. Hmmm…Peter fumed, not so much at the work he had to re-do changing the spreadsheets, but how inadequate his MBA had trained him. He remembered the book "What Havard Business School Did Not Teach You", in which street smartness, developing one's acumen was most important. He wondered where Arnold developed his skills. He got to find out from April.

After Peter and his colleagues went through the rounds of re-briefing the investment bankers, the lawyers and their public relations group of the change in strategy, it was three days past. He had been in the office day and night for one week already, and he expected another two weeks before the whole deal is wrapped up. However, once the documents were finally prepared, they had another round of discussions with Arnold. In half an hour, he told them to hold on the date of the take over until he could get the vendors to agree on the date. Arnold then went off for his round of negotiations with April in tow. Peter and his colleagues did not hear from them for two days, meanwhile it was waiting, pizza and coke, again and again. Finally the phone rang. The date is 72 hours from now. Thereafter a flurry of activities flowed, with the investment bankers, lawyers and public relations team dropping in and finalising details, going off and coming in again.

D-day came; Peter was told to bring all his documents to follow April. They went by limousine to Com-Com's headquarters, where in the board room, the previous owners and the management sat waiting for the team from Xylec. Arnold came in last, introductions were made, and then told them, "Welcome to Xylec. You are part of us now. The management team of Com-Com was stunned, but the previous owners explained that they wanted to sell off Com-Com to build a bigger and better Com-Com. The owners told them that part of the deal was that the management team would be intact without any layoffs, but there would be some changes in rules. With them, Arnold assumed Chairmanship and President of Com-Com Peter was highly anxious and excited.

The management team of Com-Com was glum but managed to smile when Arnold was introduced to them. The meeting ended with Arnold telling them that there would be a ceremony to invite all their management team on board. Peter asked April how Arnold acquired his skills. "By following his boss, just like you did"!

18   The Professional Networker ~ The First Payout

Tom managed to show 11 plans in his first month of joining, attended more than 6 meetings, and recruited one person. That person was Solomon. Henry was too busy and could not decide. The rest did not make a decision. However, Solomon bought over $300 worth of products to try. Tom persuaded Shirley to list the items he could substitute with and bought over $150 of vitamins, His neighbours heard that he was into networking and purchased some household washing items worth $50. At the 15th of the month, Tom got a check of $15. What? $15! It's a joke. He rang Paul. Paul congratulated him That is the first profit from his business. Has he ever made any money from any of his business before? Now that Paul put it in those terms, he felt better. He had never had any business on his own before. He was always a employee, and he had that mindset from school to college to graduate. Now, that's a thought. His first ever profit. He likened himself to Bill Gates and Steve Jobs who worked out of their garages and room and made his first dollar without getting it from his employer. Wow! That's good.

Keep at it and you will soon make four-figure income, Paul encouraged Tom. "We all start like this, Tom. Oh, by the way, you better photocopy that check. It will come in handy one day"

I better show this to Shirley when she comes back from work, he thought. "Ta, ra, ra! "Tom showed Shirley the $15 check. "What? Fifteen dollars?", Shirley laughed uncontrollably, "what kind of business are you in?". "Hold on, Hold on, Shirley. This is the first check from Tom Inc.", Tom reminded her, and told her what Paul told him. "Okay, let's get Alison and go to A&W to paint the town red with your first income," Shirley said sniggering away. Tom did not know whether to feel hurt or be proud. His first root beer with his first hard-earned income from HIS own business!

18   The Corporate Executive ~ The First Payout

Peter was bushed, after slaving away for three weeks in the office. His boss had been happy with the results of the takeover of Com-Com. April had been very helpful and was a very good superior, guiding him all the way. He went home to sleep.

When he woke up, it was dark and Elizabeth woke him when she switched on the hall lights. "What's up with you? ", she laughed, "you looked terrible" Peter dragged himself up from the lounge and wanted to give Elizabeth a kiss for being so understanding. "Phew! you stink.", she said unromantically, "why don't you take a shower and let's go for dinner!" "Okay, let's…" and Tom drifted away into the bathroom.

When Elizabeth had freshened herself up and waited for Peter, she was surprised that Peter came down smartly dressed in a tuxedo. "Where do you think you are going?", she asked. "To take my girlfriend and lover to the best dining place in the world," he winked at her. "For all the time you waited for me, now it's payback time!", he smiled at her and kissed her. Peter looked so handsome, cultured and romantic, and flirtatious. "Ooh…I would love to," said Elizabeth. "Ta..ra..ra! "Tom flashed a stack of $100 bills. There was a total of $2000. "We are going to have a very, very nice evening, Liz". Tom explained that the company had been driving them very hard for the past three weeks and now that the acquisition has been successful, the CEO has given everyone in the team a $2,000 advance bonus.

"Remember the Kobe beef, we wanted to try last time, but it was too expensive by the ounce? Let's try it tonight with wine. Later, let's dance and we will have a nice time in bed. Oh, after 3 weeks, I need to get attached to my bed again, and sleep, and sleep

Peter felt good about the company. He got his first payout from working so hard. Wow…this is good corporate life, he thought.

19   The Professional Networker ~ Counselling (I)

Tom began his rigorous program of showing the plan after office hours. Sometimes, it was difficult to keep up the discipline because after the office work, he would be tired. Sometimes he hears his colleague going to the pub for a drink, or he would hear some of them going to rent a video to watch for the night. However, since he has promised to work on this networking so that he can give Shirley and Alison the dream things he keeps remembering, he did not mind. Tonight, he would be seeing Lisle and her husband. After a quick dinner and a change of clothes, he drove all the 15 km to Lisle's place. He made sure of the address and the right turnings off the highway. However, when he reached Lisle's house, the lights were on, but there was no car in the porch. He waited and checked to see if he came to the right house. It was the right place. After 15 minutes, he went to the house and rang the bell. No body answered the door. He tried to look into the house though the windows. Just then a neighbour came out. "Oh, you must be Tom? Sorry to startle you. Lisle and her husband have to rush to the hospital as their child had a high fever. She called me to leave you the message. She apologised."

Tom was really down. He came all the way, but he understood the situation Lisle was in. He had once to rush Alison to a doctor as well. As he drove back, he was disheartened. He pushed the audio tape in and listened to the tape. It was a tape on counselling. He decided to call Paul. "Drop by on your way back," Paul invited. He was now out with a prospect but do wait for him in the house, he was told. He went to Paul's house and his wife, Victoria, led him in. She led him to the sitting room and gave him a soft drink, then excused himself. As he waited, he noticed several pictures and awards displayed in the room. Paul has been to Hawaii, to Las Vegas, to Alaska. Hmmm…there is the Emerald certificate, which means the Paul had at least three groups that had a steady product volume for at least 6 times in a year. That's encouraging. Paul never mentioned about his trips, but was always asking Tom about his (Tom's) business. Paul entered the room, and they chatted. Paul heard Tom's experience, and Paul asked him anyone else he had planned to see the night. Paul told Tom to always book more than one appointment since there would be bound to be cancellations.

To develop the business fast, Paul had to sometimes show plans up to 1a.m. in the night. This was concentrated work, and Paul looks forward to retiring from his full time job as a consultant in two years' time. He would have worked the networking business for five years then. Paul encouraged Tom to listen to a number of tapes, and Tom left, feeling so much better that he had someone to talk to, someone to listen and someone to counsel.

19 The Corporate Executive ~ Counselling (I)

Peter felt charged up after a good night out with Elizabeth, and they had the most enjoyable and romantic night. Life was good. He was very cheerful when he breezed into his office. He saw a message on his table. April wanted to meet up with him. He wondered what it was about. April motioned Peter to sit down and slide the report he prepared for him to look at. "Your assumptions on the financial impact of the takeover have very serious flaws," April pointed out. "We discovered this as I was going over the final numbers with Arnold. Your projections did not take into account the obsolete returned stocks, although this was quite obvious from checking with market sources. Fortunately, this was balanced out by the sale of the equipment and stocks. I think you better get the numbers right, or else!" Peter had never seen April so annoyed. He apologised and went to work immediately, even ignoring the greetings of his colleagues, who were puzzled why he was so cold that morning.

He checked and double checked the figures on his computer; there was nothing wrong. He went through the figures again, and again he found that the obsolete returned stocks were already accounted for. He was puzzled. This checking and verification went on for hours, before he realized that what he had on the computer screen and what was in the report were different versions. "Oh, no," how could this be, he moaned. He then spent the next four hours checking the figures on the computer screen and those in the report. Because so many versions of the spreadsheets were made due to later revisions, he found that different pages were compiled from different versions of the spreadsheet. He had to call for assistance. They worked until the morning to get the right version in the final report. The final figure was the same as those in the report. The mistakes self-cancelled.

The next morning, with a sleepy and gaunt face, Peter handed the final report to April who checked the figures for over an hour with Peter explaining where the mistakes were made. "Peter, you have learned a very important lesson. In this corporation, especially in corporate finance, you cannot delegate the printing of the report to your subordinates who are less experienced than you. Mistakes like this will be marked against you. As you are under my supervision, I have to take the rap for this mistake. But no more, understand?

I know you work three weeks on this report and you have so many people who are young and inexperienced. You have to learn to supervise and manage the paper and work flow." Peter nodded. He knew he got off lightly. In another less forgiving firm, he would have been fired. He needs more counsel, he decided.

19   The Professional Networker ~ Counselling (II)

Tom had fixed up a regular counselling session with Paul who told Tom that he needs to be counselled so that he in turn can learn to counsel those people he recruited. A counsellor is like a coach; because he was so deep into his network business, sometimes he cannot see the small mistakes or the correct route to take. It is similar to a coach for a professional golfer; the coach can advise the type of swing; the body turn and the right clubs to use. After a few games, the golfer needs to come back to the coach to see whether he needs to be corrected to stay on course.

Paul advised Tom that Tom should call him on everything he does and encounter, so that Paul can give him tips or third-party advice as to what he should do. For instance, Tom found out that when he was showing the plan, he made more statements than ask questions. Paul told him that like a seasoned sales person, the ratio of questions to statements should be 2:1 and not 1:3, as a novice sales person. Paul learned this in his consulting days when he followed sales persons and noted the number of times they asked questions instead of making statements to customers. Right now, Tom's questions to statements ratio was something like 1:4. He needed lots of changes.

Has Tom been listening to customers? "God gave us two ears and one mouth, so we should be listening twice as much as we talk." Paul advised. Tom nodded. No wonder when he was showing the plans, he noticed that sometimes his prospects kept yawning, or tried to do so. Maybe he needs to listen, and he can only do this if he asks more questions.

Has he been getting more people oriented? Did he know what his prospects want in life? Or has he been just showing the plans to them? Never, never talk about politics or religion. These can be distracting. Let the prospect talk, listen and then move on. Never argue and always, always agree. "You may win an argument, but you will never win a prospect. Agree with the prospect even if you disagree with his opinion, as he may have a point which is not the time to discuss". Always get the spouse involved, unless the spouse specifically requests to be excused.

Tom felt that here was Paul, whose experience was so sound and advice was so appropriate. The wonderful thing is Paul did not charge one cent for his time. It was so unlike corporate life, where those who advise will charge thousands of dollars, and those who will not, do not fancy seeing you moving ahead of the corporate ladder. There are of course few exceptions, but in this networking, Tom saw the great difference.

19   The Corporate Executive ~ Counselling (II)

Peter decided to consult some of his friends. When he had an early night, he decided to meet some of his and Elizabeth friends for a round of drinks. "Hei, Peter, we really envy you; you have a sexy girlfriend at home, and a sexy colleague at work. Want to trade places?" they all laughed. Peter wanted to make sure that Elizabeth does not get misled into thinking there was any contentious relationships at the workplace. "No, I prefer Elizabeth; she's more friendly," they all laughed. His friends have heard about April, how sexy she was, efficient but very business in her relationships with colleagues. "I would like some of your equally friendly advice," he said in jest. Then when they saw his serious look on his face, they started to quieten down and listened to him. He wanted their honest opinion as to what he should do in his work demands, which is very intense but yet needs absolute accuracy in his work.

Peter was glad he has built his network of friends that he could trust and could use as a sounding board. "Find a mentor," one suggested. He thought April would be one, but she was also his superior, and that made it difficult. "Who could he cultivate as mentor?", he wondered. "Develop a friendship with April, and seek her advice as a friend," another suggested.

"Maybe you need to supervise more, instead of doing the number crunching. You have already have more than 4 years' experience, and you are a smart ass. Why don't you choose and cultivate some trusted lieutenants? That way, you can have quality control over the work. However, you need someone play the role of the quality auditor first so that you need not be sucked into details and lose focus on the greater matter at hand?" This was Lyndon speaking. He related what happened in his place when there were so much "cock-up's that the company had to install a quality audit formally. Lyndon suggested not to have a formal auditor but to appoint someone who would play that role in every project. He thought this was the best suggestion.

"Not only that. You need to give to a third person who is not totally into detailed involvement to read the report to ensure that there is coherency and consistency in the report. Inaccuracies would be picked up by this reader. This person would also play the devil's advocate, testing every assumption you or your team put in. April should be able to play this role," another added.

Peter was glad April told him to cultivate contacts who are now friends.

20   The Professional Networker ~ Leading a Team

Taking the advice of Paul, Tom found that he could win more of his friends and prospects to become part of his network. Soon, he found that not only had he more than 20 people who became what is called his frontline, but soon they also could cultivate more networkers who became Tom's downline. Tom followed the guidance of Paul, and soon he had
- 3 to 4 active frontlines
- a total group of more than 110 people
- about half continued to listen to audio tapes
- nearly more than half attended the monthly meetings
- a quarter attended the quarterly meetings

What was more important was that although Tom purchased a regular amount of $350 of household products monthly, he was now earning a good four figure income.

He saw his income going from a few hundred dollars, to a thousand dollars and now it was three thousand dollars. This was important. After almost two years has passed, he has attained the maximum bonus from the product flow through his group. Another healthy sign was that his frontlines and down lines were also earning some money, more than the $15 he got as his first bonus check! However, his product flow was not constant and he knew that the next month, his income will fall as he has not reached a steady state yet.

That's when Paul in one of his regular counselling sessions advised Paul to learn how to lead a team and be a leader. Leadership was not easy and one cannot command or persuade people as in the workplace where there is position power and control that will make workers comply. In network building, Paul told Tom that "if he can help people get what they want, he will be able to get whatever he wants".

Paul also recommended books like "How to Win Friends and Influence People" by Dale Carnegie, and "21 Irrefutable Laws of Leadership" by John Maxwell so that Tom could be a leader. Paul also warned Tom that he needs to read "Skill with People" by Les Giblin to improve communications with his front lines, down lines, prospects and friends. He could also apply such principles in his work.

When Tom applied these principles, he found that his relationship with his team improved, and even found that Shirley was taking up the lessons in applying to their personal lives.

20   The Corporate Executive ~ Leading a Team

Peter started to pick his team that he thought would be good analysts, training them in the tricks of the trade. In addition, he would appoint more experienced staff to check on the quality of the data input, which he would verify independently from time to time. He thought his team how to produce good quality reports and rejected, on occasions many times, any reports that did not meet with the standards he expected. He also appointed a senior manager to read through the draft reports and solicited comments. This pleased the senior manager who saw his role more advisory reflecting the seniority and experience. When this was done, Peter would sit through the exercise in stages picking April's brains and letting her challenge his assumptions and his arguments. This not only improved his business relationship with her but also restored confidence and trust from her. In due course, April became less formal and more a friend.

The challenge came when Xylec had to merge Com-Com operations into its business, and yet remain entirely independent business entities. There was a apportionment of expenses for each company while independent sales were recorded. Synergies in workforce and infrastructure drove down costs and old equipment and assets that were redundant were sold. This was where Peter felt that the plan for managing the changes would have to be coordinated and April was charged with implementing the change. With the help of Peter, they have to draft a program of change, communicate the change and implement the changes. April chaired the meeting of senior managers from both companies in working out the details of the changes after Arnold had briefed on the overall vision for change: smooth, no politicking, teamwork and to be done with as little disruption as possible. He told them that April would be convening a task force for the integration of the two companies' resources, yet remain independent. April was very efficient; she picked the senior management for the task force, and Peter coopted younger staff to work out the change management plan.

Because of the authority conferred on April who then delegated the details to Peter, the program of change went very smoothly. Peter planned the dates and the details of the roll out of the programs for change. Resources required for the change were approved by April who appeared to have total control of the spending.

She would spend enormous amounts of time with Arnold, and then emerge to deliver more instructions. Peter was glad that he now had full control of his team, that he was not involved in data entry and number crunching but leading a team.

21   The Professional Networker ~Cost-Benefit Analysis

Tom now had the ideals of a dream business:
- residual income: he knew that he needs to do the business only once, and he gets paid, again and again. Just like Elvis Presley. He is dead, but his estate gets paid the royalties. The networking business allows him to earn residual income, generated when his business spawn's business leaders who earn the maximum bonus and who "breakaway" from his group as a leader of his/her own right.
- duplicable: he knew there is no limit to how much he can earn because as long as he teaches people to duplicate what he is doing in network; the potential is limitless. On his own, he has no more than 2 hours of discretionary time to build his business, but if he could develop a large network, and if there were 1000 people, he would have 2,000 hours to grow his total group business.
- global business: he knew his networking company from which he drew the products is a global company with offices in more than 80 countries. Hence, by e-mail, Tom can virtually build a network in any of those countries. That would allow him to earn money in various currency denominations, thus protecting him from recession in any country.
- willable and sellable: he could will the business proceeds to his next of kin, his wife and daughter. He knew of a couple who joined the business, but who were deceased in the 1960s. Because the network was still there, the couple were still receiving the money through their children.
- low investment and low maintenance: Tom knows of many friends who lost more than $100,000 in investments

- or start-up businesses which failed. He started this business with less than $100!

Tom knew that this business was done after office hours and his chief roles were to recruit members, train them and recommend products usage. Although it was slow at first, it is paying off. He remembers his first payout of $15, but that it would multiply many folds by duplication.

He remembers the puzzle, "would you choose to have 1 cent that doubles every day until the end of the month, or would you choose $1million now?" The 1 cent!

Even on the 10th day, the doubling would come to only $5.12, on the 15th day, $1638.40. Many would have regretted choosing the 1 cent. On the 20th day, it would be $5,242.88, and many would swear that his choice is mad. On the 25th day, however, the amount escalates to $167,772.16, and on the 31st day, it is $10.7 million!

21 The Corporate Executive ~ Cost Benefit Analysis

Peter knew that to rise through the corporation, he needs to know a number of things:
- be there before the CEO, last to leave after the CEO leaves
- detailed, yet not lose sight of the big picture. He knows that details could be used to cite specifics to his boss to demonstrate he knows his stuff.
- know what is wanted.
- numerate and good interpersonal skills.

For this, he needs to spend a lot of time acquiring those skills and interfacing with his immediate superior. That is a lot of sacrifices, staying back to work overtime to get the output on time. In return for that, he knows he can get
- high salary rises, even 25% to 30% of his salary
- perks, corporate expense, jet travel, company car
- first class hotel stays
- rapid promotion
- power through enablement
- influence through empowerment
- stock options

To achieve this, he needs to sacrifice
- time for himself and his family
- social life and

total dedication to the company's business. The only thing he was uncomfortable was that as CEO changes, he would be vulnerable and could either continue in his job, or he would have to seek new jobs. The position become more precarious when he is more senior, and he is older in age, although his technical skills and experience would be attractive to new potential employers.

In addition, his job is boss dependent; if he is able to get along with the new management, or if he is still wanted, then his job continues. He is in a pyramid situation, there is only one key position for the job, he gets it or someone else gets it. He is in a hire or fire mode, and if he works, he gets paid. If not, he will not get paid. His job scope is local, regional or international.

The maximum price is of course time. He will not be able to spend that much time with Alison, only weekends.

22 The Professional Networker ~ Emotional Roller Coasting

Tom went through periods of high emotional exhilaration and anxiety. This was caused when he had successes signing up new distributors. Nothing could describe the feeling of new people joining his network, and he could not give enough information to the new members of his group. The feeling quickly dissipated when after signing up, the members did not take as active part as they indicated or as Tom expected. Then Paul showed Tom the reasons why. And how he could improve his network. He drew a circle:

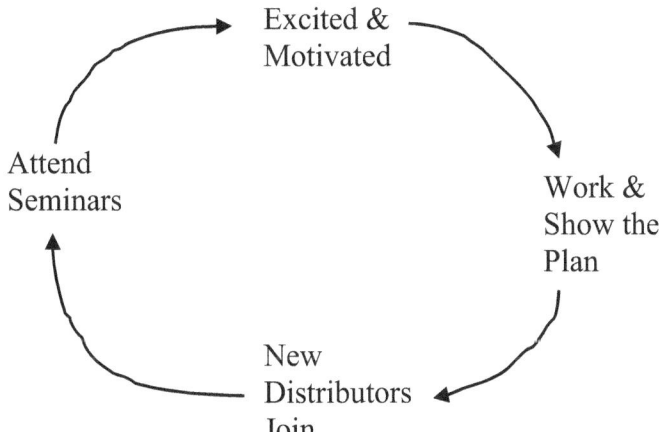

New people when they attend seminars are highly excited and motivated. That is when Tom need to quickly work on the new distributor's list and get people to join under the new distributor. As soon as the new distributor has a new downline, the new distributor will bring the new downline to attend the seminar. From one person, the numbers will double. However, if there is a break in the cycle, then what he experience will take place. Because the new distributor is unable to get a new person to sign under him/her, the interest is lost.

Paul also told Tom that once he gets a new distributor, it is not a time to relax, but a time to work even harder, as that is when the new distributor's excitement will reach an even higher level if a new downline is successfully signed on.

This is why Paul says getting new distributors is like getting a morale booster and why it is so important to keep showing the plan until he becomes financially free.

Paul also told Tom that now that he is a direct distributor, he should not wipe the sweat off his brow until he has shown enough plans to become a diamond, that is when Tom has six leaders each with enough product volume reaching maximum bonus for at least 6/12, six times in a year.

22   The Corporate Executive ~ Emotional Roller Coasting

Peter was emotionally high when he was leading his team to manage the changes brought about by the takeover of Com-Com by Xylec. Initially, the work involved interviews with so many parties and groups in both companies, that Peter felt very motivated and gung-ho about the changes. Then things began to take longer than expected. People needed training, policy and procedures needed to be re-written, compensation packages need to be equalised, redundancies were identified, and layoffs and terminations started. The employees being apprehensive whether they would be affected became careful, and less committed to their jobs. Information requested was not coming at the specified dates as persons seconded to the team became affected. Sometimes, key individuals were missing the next day and the team found out that they were being laid off.

Peter was now at an emotional low, since some of those who were made redundant were his team members and some he knew as friends. He tried to get April to intervene, but this would be seen to be unfair to other people in the company so redundancies right across the company had to be exercised. His team members became less committed and refused to work later than required. Sometimes, he had to counsel them but Peter knew it was not that easy since many had families who depended on their jobs for food and a roof over their head. A month later, when the redundancies were over, then Peter felt better. He knew his job was safe as he was handpicked by April and his corporate finance skill was badly needed in the company. Moreover, his relationship with his superior and with Arnold was very good.

With the redundancies behind them, Peter and his smaller team worked on strategies to integrate the two companies. As the redundancies were handled by April and Arnold in a separate team, Peter did not have the guilt that his team was responsible for taking away someone else's rice bowl. Very quickly, he was able to chart out strategies to

- communicate the changes in structure, roles and relationships in the two companies
- place employees in the new structures, departments and divisions in the company, & train the employees in the refined information technology and financial systems
- implement the new compensation package and incentive schemes now that the two companies are sharing marketing and sales resources

When Peter heard that April and Arnold fully endorsed the plans, he was very pleased, and emotionally returned to his previous high level.

23   The Professional Networker ~ The Next Level

Tom had to move up to the next level in the network, otherwise he knew he could not transition from his job which gives him an active income to a new lifestyle which is funded by a passive and pipeline income. At the direct distributor level, his monthly income is only about $3,000. At the emerald level, when he has three similar direct distributors, his income will be 2 ½ times. When he has six direct distributors, he knows that his income would be 6-7 times his earnings now. From thereon, the earnings would be exponential, and he knows that in certain countries, where there are enough distributors being realized within a group, the bonus alone would reach $2 million, excluding the monthly income.

Tom thought hard how he could move on the next level as he was in the level already for two years. It took him longer than expected. Meanwhile, his full-time job demands is getting tighter, and his time spent in the evenings and weekends to create a pipeline income was putting much pressure on him as he felt Shirley and Alison did not deserve to be neglected. On the other hand, he had done his self-convincing affirmation.

Hours & payout taken ~ full time job	Hours & payout taken ~ networker
9 hours per day x 5 days x 52 weeks = 2,340 hours.	3 hours x 5 days x 52 weeks + 4 hours x 2 days x 52 = 828 hours
Time taken 20 years = 46,800 hours	Time taken 5 years = 4,4140 hours
Total income, with peak of $150,000 from $50,000 per annum = $1.950 million	Total income, from 5th year on wards for 15 years, peaking at $2m from $200K per annum = $17.6 million
Total free time for family = 9 hours per day x 2 days x 52 weeks x 20 years = 18,720 hours.	Total free time for family =9 hours per day x 6 days x 52 weeks x 15 years = 42,120 hours

Tom felt that the networking business would give him 9 times more income, but it would also let him have 2 ¼ times the time to spend with his family, assuming he would still need to attend to meetings as a diamond up to 1 day a week. In addition, there are also fully paid annual trips given by the company for entering into that diamond club.

The more Tom mulled over this, the more certain he needs to move up to the next level. If he factored in the tax elements, the payout would be even greater as he can expensed out the items in running the business against tax.

23   The Corporate Executive ~ The Next Level

Peter wanted to learn as much as he could about how to do business, especially the deals in negotiating with owners or shareholders. He has heard how Arnold could talk the owners of Com-Com to sell off their shares as they have more to gain by cashing out their equity. He must move on to the next level otherwise he will always be left in managing details of business operations which would not be paid as much as he would like as a CEO. He understands the salary of CEOs could run into double digit millions if the company has a very large multimillion-dollar business. Stock options would then make the CEO very, very wealthy. He could think of the CEOs of General Electric, Sun Microsystems, IBM, etc. He dreamt about the day he would be one of the super-rich CEO, with a lot of power and authority, with a challenging job.

Right now, Peter earns $70,000 per annum, and he was given 3 months bonus for his hard work. After taxes, he felt there was not much left to save and buy his own property. He was fortunate that he was given a company car, the expenses of which was fully borne by the company. That would put him in the $100,000 category, if he factored in the equivalent for car and bonuses. Not bad for a 5-year post-graduate. He expected much higher as he had an MBA, but his rise in salary was curtailed as his previous boss left for a better position and he did not get the promotion he wanted.

How could he move on to the next level. He started to work out his earnings potential: Peter knew that he could be wealthy if he performed, if he could be the number 1. However, he will have very little time for his family, which would be during the vacation, many of which were spoiled by call backs by the company or by hitching on assignments to places that he was taking his vacation. If he is number 2, he will be less wealthy but still comfortable. He must learn to be Number 1.

Projected Earnings Potential

At $100,000 pay, assuming he gets average increment of 20% and promotion of at least 50% every 5 years, his earnings would be
= $259,200 5th year
= $806,215 10th year
= $2.5 million 15th year.
Total gross earnings for career = $10.8 million
Stock options could be between $5million - $10 million

Time with family = 14 days' vacation x 8 hours x 15 years = 1,680 hours

24 The Professional Networker ~ Self Affirmation

Tom counselled with Paul. It was fortunate that Tom had a good mentor, a good upline who would advise him how to proceed forward. It's like being in a minefield and Paul is there first de-mining all the danger spots so that he, Tom, could follow Paul safely across, by depending on Paul's experience. Paul is also following his leader, who has a much larger business and that experience is helping Paul to become a leader himself to move up.

Paul told Tom to qualify for the leadership seminar which would hold overseas so that he (Tom) could meet up with the global leaders and develop a world vision of the enormous size of the global business. That seminar would also help Tom to visualise how he could develop his business by associating with some of the most successful and positive network leaders in the world. This seminar was an annual affair, opened only to those who qualified to attend. Tom had been to one "Go Diamond" meeting by qualifying for the maximum bonus level. Since then, he has qualified annually until he became a direct distributor. The experience was very motivating for him as it was not only a seminar, but also a holiday as there was sufficient money from the bonus to pay for the whole trip overseas, with excess for shopping, which Shirley loved.

For this leadership seminar, Tom was told to qualify as an Emerald, which means he has to work out which people in his group that he can develop as leaders and as direct distributors, with business volume that is steady at least for six months in a year (6/12). The mind set, Paul told Tom, is not whether he has three persons who are ready to move forward, but whether Tom's is ready to move forward. With that mind set, he can then work his plans to achieve the goals.

For this change, Tom has to elevate his mind to a new level of confidence and thinking. He has to affirm himself every day in front of the mirror that he is going Emerald to move to Diamond. More audio tapes on success stories of achievers and more tips of growing a bigger business. Read the right books, and for that, Tom read the "Magic of Thinking Big" again. His list of prospects has to be expanded. He needs to be more disciplined in showing more plans and following up on

prospects that he has shown plans.

He must also be more persuasive and resolute in getting more people to the quarterly three-day "weekend leadership seminar". More counselling is needed, both for him, his frontlines and his downlines. After a month, he felt so much more charged up. From one of the diamonds, he also learned how to build up his stamina by exercise.

24   The Corporate Executive ~ Self Affirmation

Peter did some research and started to list down people who could become his mentor in his career. They could be anyone who was successful and influential, with sufficient corporate experience who could guide him. He tracked down 3 persons who seemed likely candidates who could help him. One of them, Stanley, was a board member of a manufacturing company and is now a venture capitalist. He therefore has exposure to many companies. Stanley was a father of one his classmates in high school.

After a few weeks, he managed to convince Stanley because he would be a good mentor for him. Stanley was in his late fifties, a fatherly figure, who likes to be low profile in his business community. He likes a game of golf during weekdays and keeps off the course on weekends, as he dislikes crowds and waiting time to play. Stanley would be his off-office mentor while April would be his in-office mentor.

Stanley advised Peter to buy magazines on CEOs and businesses. He recommended "Fortune" magazine as the articles are very readable and interesting. It also gave insights into businesses. However, he warned Stanley that the articles depended on the writers who may be familiar with certain industries but not all. Read as widely as possible. "Havard Business Review" is also a good journal as the articles are not too academic but gives new ideas that is already in practised. The best was for him to join and fraternize CEOs in "CEO Clubs" or "Directors' Clubs". Social and golf clubs are also good place to get in touch closely with people that you may not normally associate with in business gatherings. Stanley often avoided unimportant cocktail parties by certain companies as "sales persons and personal investor advisers" frequent them. Peter had a long chat with Stanley that lasted into the wee hours of the morning.

He learned from Stanley that sometimes spouses and girlfriends are good advisers as well as they would approach the business problem from the non-business but people viewpoint. Hence, communication, interpersonal skills and diplomacy became the key points.

Stanley told Peter that sometimes it is better not to mention a mistake done by a gentleman or lady than to point out, as "frankness will never get you anywhere but niceties will get you everywhere".

"Tell yourself you are CEO material, therefore, move on to more important issues rather than delve on nitty gritty mistakes. Learn from one's folly and be generous with praises. Learn how to say, "I am sorry", and listen to people. However, be firm."

25   The Professional Networker ~ Preparation

Tom had read how one of the best salespeople, Zig Ziglar, in his book "See You At the Top", went to see his doctor. After the medical examination, Zig was told that he looked fine for a man of fifty-five. "I beg your pardon," Zig said, "I am only forty-five". The condition of Zig made him start to jog on a regular basis. In the beginning, it was tough. He could not even run one block. Then panting and wheezing, he tried again the next day, and the next, and the next. Soon, Zig was running not only blocks, but also miles. Ten years later, Zig went to have his medical examination. The doctor pronounced him fit, very fit, for a man of forty-five! That discipline of exercise changed him.

Tom started to take a whole battery of vitamins, and started to manage his diet. He avoided high fats, high sugar and high carbohydrate foods. Food with fiber, and fruits were included with every meal. Shirley and Alison followed Tom in his daily regime to build up his stamina. Tom started exercising in the gym, and then moved on to jogging. He drank plenty of water, and ensured that he took lots of antioxidants (lecithin with vitamin E, vitamin C and beta carotene) and multivitamins, because during office, he had to skip meals. He also took high protein diet, and supplemented his diet with protein powder. Shampoo was chosen to ensure that the right type was used for his hair. He bought a water filter that could remove polycarbons, insecticides and pesticides, together with toxic metals. High sugar carbonated drinks were replaced with natural fruit juices. He made sure that he had a regular meal that was balanced. He found that most of these items were sold by the company that he is building his network on. By doing this, he not only saved money, but he could also build up his personal sales volume by self-consumption.

Daily, he read positive books and avoided making negative statements. When there were doom and gloom talk in his office because the economy was slow, Tom cheered them up by avoiding talking about such news but moved on to items that had humour or had positive impact on everybody.

He woke up and faced himself in the mirror, "a diamond is in the making". Now he is ready to move.

25   The Corporate Executive ~ Preparation

Peter made a special trip to the largest book store, browsed through the magazine racks and the self-improvement shelves, bought the recommended magazines and books, and started to read them in his spare time in the office and at home. Sharing the information with his colleagues boosted the morale of everyone in the team. They have never seen Peter so cheerful. Peter also avoided rushing straight into business discussions without initially enquiring how his colleagues are. That way, he became more friendly and meetings took off much better than in the past.

When he had time, he invited his colleagues for lunch for a chat without talking business. He went with April for lunch on several occasions. He found her very approachable and open about herself. He never had a conversation with her before, only straight business talk. He liked her even better, and she was now more relaxed, more helpful, less business-like. Given any small opportunity, he tried to chat with Arnold, but the exchange was always short, as office staff wanting Arnold to sign documents or make decisions on his meeting schedules always interrupted him.

Besides making the rounds of social events among business friends, he now picked and choose which to go and which to miss, as he looked to CEO and directors' clubs' events and meetings.

In work, although he would be friendlier, Peter was always firm in deadlines, quality of reports and information, and meeting objectives of the exercise or projects. With his better interpersonal skills, and admission of mistakes, but insistence on quality results, Peter developed a following among the younger executives, and the older more senior staff began to prefer him to handle business matters on their behalf. Peter also ws more disciplined. Where there was not much work for the day, he would insist that his subordinates go home earlier, but make up for it when work load was crazy and demanding.

All the while, Peter would confer with Stanley if he were not sure, and checked with April, in company issues. Sometimes he would use both as sounding board for his plans and proposals that he has been asked to craft.

Using the two inputs, he found that he could get even better solutions. He also stopped giving solutions for his staff, but trained them to come up with the solutions, although he would hint at the outcome.

26   The Professional Networker ~ Reasons

Tom knew each of the steps he had to take and these were the reasons he learned why each was important:
- Dream ~ this was self-actualization of the hierarchy of needs expounded by the management guru, Maslow, who theorized that human beings have a hierarchy of needs which includes basic physiological needs of warmth, shelter and food (Abraham Maslow, *Motivation and Personality, 1954)*. Once these are met, others emerge to dominate. Next are social or level needs, and ego or self-esteem needs. On self-actualization level, the individuals achieve their own personal potential. This is the driver of the business.
- List ~everyone has connections and the purpose is to convert these into income producing assets.
- STP ~ Show the Plan is equivalent to work. Although many view this as demeaning, it can become a habit. Nakajima, the legendary network builder in Japan, and who drives a Porche to work his business, developed this into a habit that he never stops showing the plan even as he flies from Japan to USA for meetings. The reason was that this habit made him a multimillionaire.
- Tape ~ it is expensive to have mentors to be with you all the time and this medium is to be able to duplicate the mentoring and teaching, and also have access to the mentors and coaches 24 hours and globally.
- Books ~ With the maxim the "leaders are readers", reading books help to shape and develop positive mind-sets that think big.
- Products and Customers ~ this is the source of the income. When customers use the products, they continuously use the products when they are satisfied that the products are quality, safe
-

biologically and environmentally, and are necessary in recession or buoyant economies.
- Functions ~ weekly, monthly and quarterly meetings enable distributors to not only be motivated, but also to share experiences from the achievers and the leaders.
- Teamwork ~ teams by working for the common goal, strengthen each other, help to duplicate the networking, so that the leaders can find someone better than them that can duplicate them.

26   The Corporate Executive ~ Reasons

Peter knew that to be ahead he had reasons for the activities he had to pursue:

- Goals ~ To be at the top, he must make sure that he meets company's goals and objectives. This will confer upon him position power.
- Network ~ He must know who are influencers, supporters and leaders that he can rely on to move up the corporate ladder.
- Company Plans and Proposals ~ He had to produce these Plans and Proposals, many of which need to be modified, changed and rejected before he is given the free hand to develop his own plans and proposals that will be adopted by the company.
- Tapes ~ The company had many tools to further his personal development. In addition, he dictated many tapes for his secretary to type. This was however a dying practice which is substituted by managers typing their own memos in the form of emails.
- Books ~ There are many "how to" books used in companies, including SOPs, "standard operating procedures" that Peter had to follow.
- Products, Services and Customers ~ Customers are the life of the company; in service companies, trust and belief are the most important. Arthur Andersen, one of the oldest accounting firm, disintegrated and broke up when that trust in its service was broken by its role in the Enron scandal (the accounting irregularities were not picked up by AA but which further attempted to hide the malpractice).
- Functions ~ Business functions are to promote the company and its services. Training and development are also functions that are deemed important to develop the human capital of the organisation.
-

- Teamwork ~ Although there is much talk about individualism and collectivism in companies, American companies tend to be individualistic (everyone is an individual and culture caters to the promotion of the individual) while Asian companies tend to be collectivistic (the group is more important than the individual). In practice, teamwork is not easily inculcated as a culture.

27 The Professional Networker ~ Action Time, or is it?

Tom started a series of daily deliberate actions (DDA) to help to prime him for the network building activities, which would demand a lot of stamina and energy from him. He started to jog regularly, by running in the evenings immediately after work. It was hard work; before he could even run a round of the jogging track, he was already panting. His sweat was dripping from his body like water springing a leak from a sponge. He stopped after one round of jogging and one round of walking. That night before he went to bed he found that his joints ached like never before. The worse that was that he had not even shown one plan that night.

That night he checked his DDA list:
- Have you shown any plans today?   No!
- Have you listened to 2-3 tapes today?   No!
- Have you met one new frontline today?   Yes.
- Have you reviewed your Focus Board (activity) today? No!
- Have you done something at the bottom of each leg?   No!
- Have you read a book on goal setting or people skills? Yes
- Have you exercised 20 minutes today?   Yes
- Have you reviewed your goals and affirmation today?   Yes
- Have you used the system of edification today?   Yes
- Have you taken your multivitamin today?   Yes
- Have you drank sufficient water today?   Yes
- Have you influenced someone positively today?   No

Tom was told that the biggest creativity everyday was to stay focused on these basics. He knew he must improve, so he consciously started to adhere to these principles to set him financially and time free from his 9-5 job. There would be challenges that would deter him from achieving his goal but he was determined that he would succeed.

27   The Corporate Executive ~ Action Time, or is it?

Peter had fixed up a series of power lunch appointments, which would put him in touch with many executives and acquaintances. Initially it went well. However, after a number of lunches for Mondays to Thursdays, he found that it was getting too expensive on his pocket. Since he was inviting others for lunch, his lunch dates thought he was paying. On Friday, he noted that the bill for lunch was already topping $100! and there was still Friday to go. Although he knew his company would pick up the entertainment expenses, he could not claim for lunch every day. It would be unethical. Although nobody would question his claims, he was not in the business development function and continuing to submit lunch claims would not get him into good stead with his bosses.

Work was also accumulating for the following week. How could he carry on the lunchtime arrangements to network or increase his knowledge of city business through this means? He tried to arrange for appointments immediately after work. Then, he could not be seen to be going off early. The other plan was to meet them for a drink and then return to office. That would force him to remain even later in the office. Moreover, his business contact was always busy and was not available for drinks, except on Fridays. It was proving harder than he thought.

He sought the advice of Stanley. "Do it at all odd and even times," he said. "Breakfast meetings? Dinners? Early lunch? Teatime? But avoid liquor, except in the evenings. Management may think poorly of you if you reek of liquor during office hours. Weekends. Sometimes, this may require you to drive a long distance so that the venue is convenient for both. Musical evenings or stage shows. Not necessary meal times contacts. Develop relationships, rather than very formal settings. Even a ball game would help. Be upfront and split the bill. They will understand. Have social activities around your business activities. However, be careful not to intrude into your family time. Too much and your family will complain."

So, Peter started to arrange his contacts with friends and associates and involved Elizabeth too. Elizabeth was not always free as she too had work to complete late into the evenings in the office, but she would try whenever she could. This worked well for a week and Peter had to adjust his timing and appointments again until he could make this a routine, fitting the demands of his work.

28   The Professional Networker ~ 7 Logical Reasons

Tom learned that there are 7 logical reasons why people would get into the business and he need to master the presentations:
- Gearing: in business, if the borrowing/capital is >2, it means don't lend. If more than 2 times for personal gearing (e.g. credit card), it means highly geared. Hence, there is a good reason to do this business.
- Inflation: even if one has saved lots of money, inflation will reduce the purchasing power. For comparison

Expenses	1998	2002	Inflation
Starting Salary	$3,500	$4,000	14.3%
Basic Car	$28K	$56K	200%
Movies	$2	$6	300%
Coffee	$1	$4.50	450%
University	$4,500	$12,000	800%

While the cost of goods has gone up, the salary has not even doubled.
- The business could enable them to earn $20,000 per month. There are 3 options for an individual

	Work	Own Profession	Network
Retirement Age	55 years	60 years	30-35 years
Annual Leave	14-30 days	2-3 days	2-11 months
Qualifications	Degree	Degree or better	Dream
Investment	4 years for degree	$0.5 –$1.0 m	$100 + $3,600

| Income on Retirement | Pension, or zero | 30% decrease | Income reduces by only 1% |
| On death | nil | nil | 85% pass to next of kin |

The networking business can generate a perpetual income.
- It takes more hours to work a lifetime than the hours needed for networking business.
- The business caters to the purchase of necessities. In real life situation, about 90% of salary is used for consumables (food, household items). Only 10%, and if there is sufficient, of the salary is used for investment or insurance. Hence, catering to the necessities segment has more opportunities.
- Anybody trained in the system of networking building can make it as a predictable system is used.
- A highly rated company (e.g. triple A rating) like Amway has no debts and therefore bankruptcy is highly unlikely.

28   The Corporate Executive ~ Logical Reasons To Be An Executive

Peter's training in business is to be an efficient executive, but the training is to be an employee. These are the reasons why he strives so hard to succeed in this position:

- He is trained in business administration and it is logical to work for experience and move up the career path.
- Most of his colleagues move along the same stream of activity, get a job and that is part of the cycle for almost all his classmates. Only a few get into business, because of family and friends' influences or because of circumstances.
- Getting a salary at the end of the month, that will buy food and accommodation is a natural habit of many adults.
- He has been reading and dreaming of the corporate executive life and now that he is in it, he naturally relishes the realisation of his ambition. However, sometimes he feels that he has no options.
- Following his parents' footsteps, he naturally got a job and work.
- Influence of recruiting agents from companies who do their usual "milk rounds" of universities and recruit them.
- If he does not become an executive, what will he do?

Peter reminisces how he got into his job and he felt that was the only logical way to work. What else is he mentally prepared for? Unlike medical doctors, lawyers, architects, they will eventually have their own firms or be partners in their profession. Hence, Peter worked as hard as he could to be a successful executive, then become the senior executive and hopefully, if he can cut it, to be a CEO.

29 The Professional Networker ~ 7 Emotional Reasons Why People Do Not Do This Business

Tom also realized that people will not do this business because of these emotional reasons.

- Ego ~ not many can put their ego away and work in building this business after their office work hours, especially if they do not see the future reward, as they will get paid again, again and again once they have built the network.
- Too much work ~ many consider this meeting up with many people as too much work.
- Children~ many see the children as the obstacle to doing this business as they say they have no time. So, they take care of the children, but spent more time in front of the television, while watching the children play. Children should be the reason why this business should be built.
- Making Use of their Friends ~many see network building as making use of their friends. Helping a friend succeed is the only reason you can succeed, not making use of friends.
- Believe That This Business is Too Materialistic ~ This business generates money to resolve many problems, rather than making money as the end in mind. Many networkers have given their money to help just causes. One networker has given music scholarships to the talented musically but financially poor students. The money was also donated to finance the running of a children hospital in India. Another has donated and raised much money to distribute food and medicine to the needy in Afghanistan and other countries via a charity, Mercy Corp.
- No Time ~ the most usual reason. You have to invest time to create time.
- Cannot Do It ~ Not enough belief. The dream will drive many to succeed.

29   The Corporate Executive ~ 7 Emotional Reasons Why People Do Not Succeed in Corporations

Peter knew that to work in corporations require a certain mindset which may not fit with everybody's ideal of a work place. There are certain reasons why this is so:
- Cannot Work Under Supervision ~ some individuals like the freedom to work and act without supervision or the need for reporting. Working under a boss do not appeal to them and these individuals often have frequent job changes while rising in rank in their jobs.
- Know Better than Superior ~ although right or wrong, individuals may not feel that their superior know or is more experienced than them. Hence, there is always dissatisfaction that they should be their own boss without a superior.
- Pride and Ego ~ not all bosses are good managers or have good people relationship qualities. Individuals may have their pride or ego bruised or hurt by superiors and vowed never to work in a corporation.
- Corporate Culture ~ some corporations have a very strong culture and policy about working. There are certain rules and regulations that may not allow employees to do, such as pursuing a second source of income from a trade that may conflict with the interest of the company. It takes some effort to accept the culture, hence there are staff turnover when one company takes over another as the new culture may clash with the accepted and known culture one has worked with for years. Dress code in companies may dictate certain types of dress while in another company, the dress code may be very relaxed. Microsoft and IT companies are known to tolerate informal office wear while the more traditional companies would require business shirt and tie.
-

- Room for growth ~ it is not easy to work in a company that will not allow personal growth, although most companies now look at the individual and personal development as part of the career planning in the organisation. An employee may feel that there is no room for growth while another may perceive there is plenty of development potential.
- Equity in compensation ~ it is not the absolute amount but the equity in compensation that makes a person leave the company.
- Network. Every company has its own inner temple of employees, and a person may feel left out and therefore leave the company.

Peter feels that many of these reasons are more emotional than logical why people drop out of the corporate lifecycle. So far, it has not affected him.

30 The Professional Networker ~Key Success Factor

Tom knew what were the key success factor that contribute to his

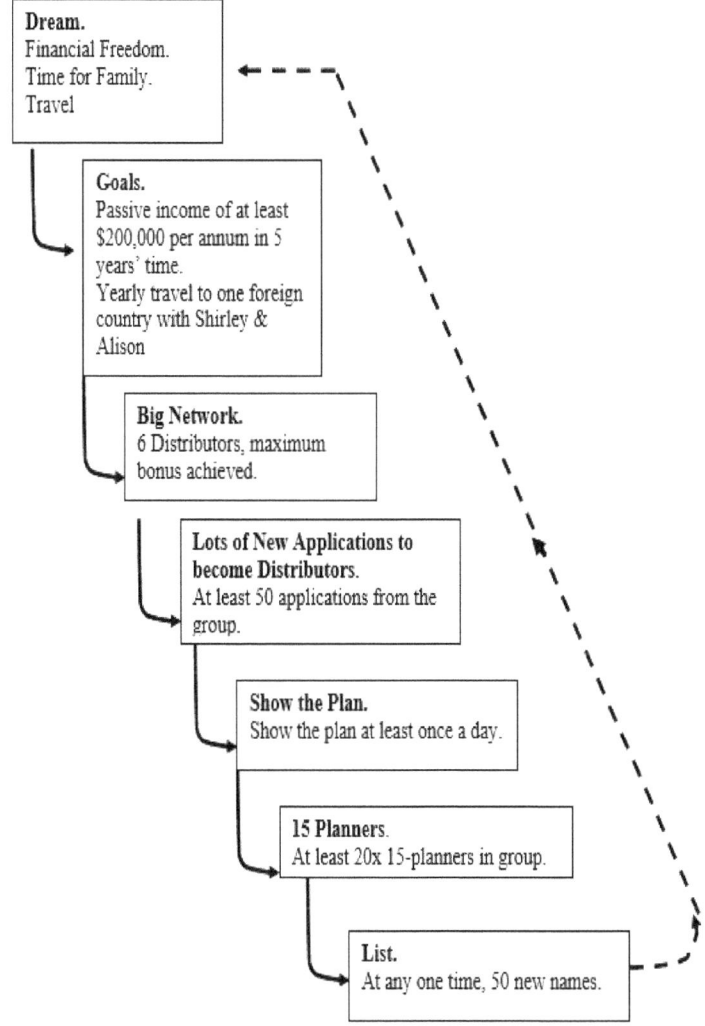

dream:

Tom's dream and goal has to start with a big list, which needs updating every day, so that he can continue show the plan, have people who would like to develop the business with their dreams and show at least 15 plans a month. That way, with a common goal by at least twenty 15 planners, new applications to join as distributors would grow by duplication. Tom needs to look for 6 good men/women who he can help to share and jointly help them to achieve their dream so that he can achieve his dream.

30 The Corporate Executive ~ Key Success Factors

Peter has worked his guts out but so far; he has not moved as quickly as he would like. He sat down and started to analyse the key success factors to reach his goal as CEO.

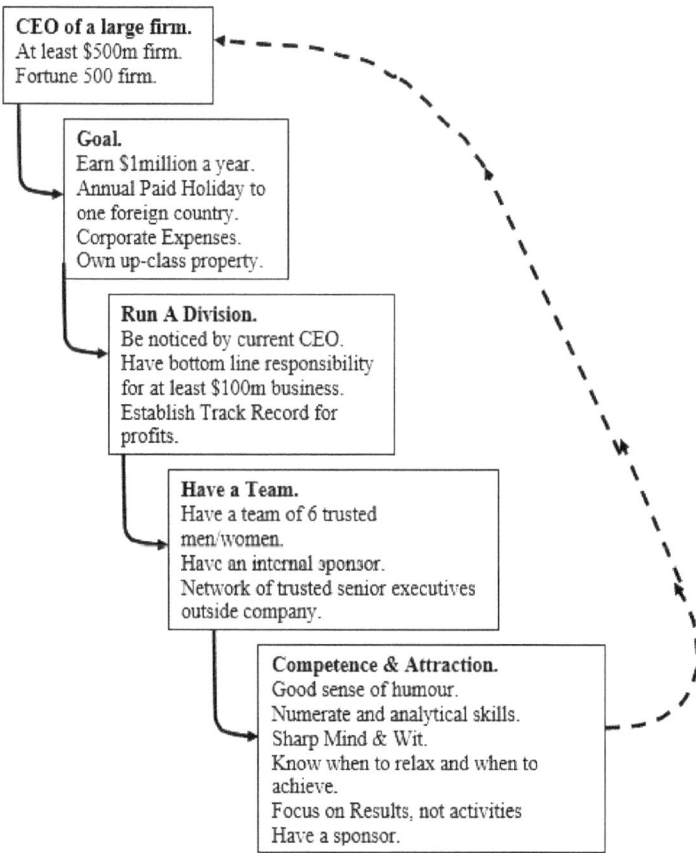

Peter knows that even though he has all the skills and knowledge, without an internal sponsor, he will never be able to make break through the ranks and get noticed by the CEO. April would be a good sponsor, but in his position in the staff function not in the line function, that would be difficult for her. He started to now move away from activities that would not help him achieve his goals.

31   The Professional Networker ~ In the Thick of It!

Tom has built up his contact list and constantly adding new names to it. He also started to prioritise his network building by focusing on the showing of the business plan around his work, rather than the other way round. He was cancelling his appointments to show the plan when he had extra work or meeting. Now, he gave his first priority to plan showing, unless he could not avoid it. He also made appointments based on the time-blocks that he made:

Time	Monday	Tuesday	Wednesday	Thursday	Friday	Saturday	Sunday
8am							
10am							
12n	W	O	R	K			
2pm							
4pm							
6pm							
7pm							
8pm			PLAN SHOWING				
9pm							
10pm							
11pm							

With these time-blocks, Tom knew that he could at least show 3 plans in the weeknights and at least 6 plans over the weekends, and still have time to spend with his family. As the number of plans he showed would bring him the freedom he desired, he was keen to show as many plans as possible because he did a simple calculation that convinced him that it was a numbers game he need to win:

To be a diamond, he needs to show 1,000 plans.

10 plans a month=120 plans a year =8-9 years to be free.
1 plan a day=365 plans a year= takes him 3 years to be free.
3 plans a day=1095 plans a year=take him 1 year to be free.
Practical: 2 plans a day x 220 days = 440 plans a year=2.5 years
to be free.

As Tom knew that over-optimism will lead to burn-up and kill his enthusiasm, and pessimism will kill his dream, he opted for the optimal plan showing of at least 2 plans a day for the year, with days that he is unable to show plans due to many reasons (sick, off, work spilling into evenings or weekends, family reasons). He will start by making one appointment a day and then move up to the pace of 2 appointments per day, his comfortable level.

31 The Corporate Executive ~In the Thick of It!

Peter started to analyse and shift his time to give him better time management:

Time Per day: Now	Time Per Day: Plan
Meetings = 2 hours Planning = 1 hour Administration=2.5 hours Work (paper, report) = 2 hours Travel (to and from) = 1.5 hours Lunch = 1 hour Functions = 1 hour **Total=11 hours**	Meetings = 1 hour Planning = 1 hour Administration=1 hour Work on results=3 hours Travel (to and from) =1.5 hours Lunch & Functions=1 hour Meet with Mentor= 0.5 hours Personal development=2 hours **Total = 11 hours**

He would spread his time focusing on results, counselling with his mentor and developing & honing his interpersonal skills and competencies daily. His personal development would include learning from senior executives, reading and working what he learned daily into his work.

He avoided wasteful time in meetings and chitchat so that he could have more time working on activities that will produce better reports and proposals. He also spent more time learning about other departments' activities hoping that he could get into line management to prove his capabilities. When he spots any opportunities, he would volunteer for the work. This led him to produce even better reports. He has told April of his intention and April has no objection as long as the company has the best person for the job.

He kept an eye on business development as this would enable him to startup businesses as well as evaluate businesses for viability, which is part of his job anyway, but he did not have any chance for starting up businesses.

31   The Professional Networker ~ In the Thick of It! (II)

Tom showed the network business plan to a Senior Vice President of a software engineering company that was based in Chicago, with sales aimed at international markets, especially China and the Far East. A dinner appointment was made the day before and at 6 in the evening they met. Kenneth was still a bachelor, engaged to an educator, who was already a member of another network marketing company. Kenneth was open but he was not so keen as he was quite comfortable in his position. Moreover, he holds about 3% shares in this small company. His software expertise and knowledge allowed him the shareholding.

Tom asked Kenneth what would he do if he had both time and money. Kenneth without hesitating said he would get into business, a trading business. Tom was surprised as Kenneth joined his present company from an academic institution as a physicist who learned finance because of the mathematical and equations involved in financial modelling. Kenneth was also interested to travel. He agreed that his present job would not allow him a perpetual income which the network business would. The business risk in network building was almost negligible compared to the financial investment required for a conventional business. Tom explained how by being a member of the network, he could order products via the internet. The products were necessities; hence in recession or in a buoyant economy, they were being used. By shopping from the company, it was possible to build a passive income that would be generated from Kenneth's assets, which would be his network of contacts and friends. Kenneth however has a hang-up on network building as his aunty used to be involved in direct selling of household products. Tom assured him that the system of generating sales now was by referral and substitution of his consumption from supermarket sources to the internet sources. Except for fresh meat and vegetables, he could shop for whatever products he wishes.

Tom also learned that Kenneth had workers who knew people in India that he could recruit as members and add to his (Kenneth's) network. Tom showed Kenneth the financial freedom that he could gain. He illustrated this by turning to the pages of homes that successful distributors owned.

There were also pictures of vacation sites around the world, and of cars that financial freedom could buy. Kenneth requested for the websites that featured the products and Tom's personal website. Tom wrote these on his own personal name card which he gave to Kenneth who promised he will get back to Tom. "Will he join?" Tom wondered. As they parted, Tom realized he did not ask enough questions!

31 The Corporate Executive ~ In the Thick of It! (II)

Peter implemented his new time management plan so that he spent less time on administrative and meeting chores, but focused on results-oriented activities. He also consulted his mentor more often and invited friends and contacts to develop himself personally, after reading self-improvement books.

He spent sometime in the marketing department learning about the communication and computer equipment the company was handling. Each of the sales team had a number of key accounts, and was supported by the marketing and technical support team to push the sales. The marketing cycle was quite long, and often after the initial contact was made, sales was generated after a year, and the purchasing of such equipment was a major capital expense item which has to be approved during the annual budget cycle of companies. Leading to the event when the actual sales proposal was put in, there had to be product introductions and demonstration of the products. Peter followed the sales and marketing team to understand the processes involved and also to learn the issues that were usually brought up by the customers. The usual items mentioned were the balance between customisation, cost and off-the-shelf products. Customisation raises the costs of purchase and maintenance of the computer system, and also replacement of the software and hardware as updates were quite frequent due to the technology upgrading. Peter followed the sales team a number of times and checked with the marketing team of the positioning of their products against the competitors and the image of the company as a supplier. In both scores (image and positioning), the company was rated high. However, cost of customised system to the customer was a problem. Upgrading was also a problem.

Peter started to think deeply into these problems as sales hinged upon competitiveness of the package and not just on technical superiority. Xylec was not as well-known as IBM or HP, but its systems were just as costly to the customer. Analyses showed that Xylec and Com-Com costs were high as both companies did not have proprietary products but bought components from other companies and assembled with customisation. Sometimes the software customisation had to use outside software houses to complete the tasks.

The service component made Xylec and Com-Com less competitive. Hmmm…what about offering outsourcing services as other companies have done. That would enable Xylec and Com-Com to have long-term contracts and income while operating the IT and communication services to companies. That would make sense. Hmm.

32   The Professional Networker ~ What is My Priority?

Tom used to make sure he would complete his office work first before he gave any time to his networking business. Now he made sure that the first thing he did in his office was to organise his office work around this networking activities. He used to make appointments to show the plan after he has fitted all his work meetings and appointments, and then when he has time, he would fit in the network appointments in the evenings. Sometimes, when he was held up in the office, he would call his prospects and change the time or date. Now that the network has become his passport to freedom, he would even leave the office early, or defer the completion of his office work or meeting to the next day. If he has a major function in the evening for his network business, he would ensure that a few days before, he would arrange his office work and appointments so that there was no clash in his priorities.

In this manner, Tom was able to show at least 1 plan a day, and sometimes, even 3 plans when he is able to make the appointments. As a result of this re-arrangement, he was able to sponsor more people as his frontline, which would lead him closer to his goal to seek 7 good men/women who could share his vision of partnering to be financially and time free. Sometimes, unexpected things do happen.

On Thursday, Tom had already made appointments to meet two new prospects at a hotel where the network was going to hold its weekly business opportunity presentations. Tom would meet them at the function room at 7.30p.m. and planned to leave early to his home, so that he can freshen up with a shower and a change of clothes, including wearing his business suit at the function. Everything was planned and he had arranged to have a quick dinner in the house with

Shirley. At 4p.m. a crisis happened. The government officials from the Trade Department were inspecting his company, Food Manufacturing Enterprise over some returns of goods sold and changes in the sales reported for the month. Tom was told to meet up in the conference room in the factory's premise, which was about 2 kilometres away. His Chief Executive was to answer and meet with the trade officials. Tom and his division chief arrived first to confer with the senior executives of the factory, and immediately action was drawn up to review all the relevant sales contracts, documents and invoices.

A crisis management plan was formed. Tom had to digest all the materials and brief the Chief before meeting with the officials. Tom dug into the materials, and then started to diagnose the problems at hand, and suggest a solution. It was now 5 p.m. and Tom became very nervous that he would miss his appointments.

32   The Corporate Executive ~ What is My Priority?

Peter suggested to April and to Arnold to change the business concept for Xylec and Com-Com from just offering products and software solution services to outsourcing services. Many banks and companies have outsourced their IT departments and support services to companies like Accenture and IBM. Xylec and Com-Com, taking the strategic synergies of both companies and beefing up on its software competencies, could form outsourcing services as the new products to be offered to clients. This would be a multimillion business and ensure long-term income for the two companies. Although without expertise, Peter thinks that there are already inhouse expertise that the companies can start with. As firms start to shrink its core employees, the support functions will be outsourced. The only difference is that Xylec and Com-Com would be the outsourcing firms to the companies offering IT outsourcing services and to companies that uses large server and communications network. The challenge is to get its first customer and then the business could build up from there. If this does not work, Peter assured April and Arnold, the people could then be transferred back to their current positions and operating units.

April and Arnold nodded in agreement. "Why don't you come up with a proposal with you as the CEO of the division? However, if this fails, the unit will be cut off, including all the people. We cannot have failures. So the best option is to burn the bridges. When the Spaniards invaded South America, that was what the captain did to their ships. Are you game on this, Peter?", Arnold put to him. Peter was excited over the challenge. Here was an opportunity to be CEO. "I'll put up the papers and propose how we can get there." "Remember, Peter, we always believe in numbers. Financial numbers persuade, qualitative statements assuage, and outsourcing will be the message!", Arnold smiled. Though a tough man, Arnold was also a shrewd man who would support his uttermost support if he finds the subordinate worthy.

Peter immediately started towards his "den" in the office, and started to think how to make this work. This was what he was waiting for, an opportunity to move up. April was eager for this project to happen, as she was responsible for bringing Peter to Arnold's attention. "It has all the right things in place, the timing, the skills and knowledge and the financial support. hmm. How do we get the first customer.

Would an outsourcing firm outsource its own networks to this company?" This would be my priority now.

33 The Professional Networker ~ Clash of Priorities

When he had a chance, Tom went to a quiet place and contacted his mentor and upline, Paul. He doubts he can make the appointment and wanted to cancel his prospects attending the meeting. Paul told Tom not to worry, as the system of network was to rely on the system and not on people. Paul would look out for Tom's two prospects and take care of them. Tom was to concentrate on doing a good job in his office, Paul told him.

With that worry taken away, Tom could focus on the problem at hand. He was glad that this business network had a lot of help from his upline to assist, which was quite different from his job, when he could not delegate, and he must personally attend to the matter at hand. Digging deeper into the stack of documents, Tom found that customer Zilon had a regular pattern of purchasing, accepting delivery of the goods and sending back about 30% of the goods on a quarterly basis. He wondered why this was so. Some whistle-blower in Zilon had tipped off the trade officials about this irregular practice which therefore distorted the true sales figures, especially during the last quarter of the year when companies generally tried to push sales in order to beat the sales forecasts. As Zilon was a public listed company, trade officials frown upon this practice as an artificial way of meeting targets, and therefore contravened true declaration of sales. Zilon was suspected of manipulating its business figures and therefore its profits to keep its stock price up. The whistle-blower had a grievance over Zilon which has renegaded on its incentive to the employee. Tom was relieved that Food Manufacturing was not the suspect in this sales rigging but the trade officials wanted evidence that this was happening in Zilon. Food Manufacturing was just a supplier of communication products and was not a party to Zilon's deception. Tom relayed this information to his division chief who by now was also aware of the regular shipments back to Food Manufacturing, which has been taking place for a long time. His CEO was quickly briefed over the situation, and the division chief assured him that this was a matter that he could handle. There was no crisis as originally thought. Food Manufacturing was the supplier and would be needed to testify before the trade commission. With that, the CEO ordered a clean-up of all such acts.

Tom and his division chief. Tom knew he would need a month meeting up with customers and suppliers and informing them of new regulations in the company that forbade such a huge amount of ship backs. Some companies would be prosecuted for trade manipulation. Tom was relieved that Paul was there to help him over his priorities.

33   The Corporate Executive ~ Clash of Priorities

Peter wrote out his business concept and plan. To experiment with outsourcing, he needs to persuade some key executives and technical experts to join him work out his concepts. He is a very likeable person but many were not sure of him as a team leader. He chose 7 good persons: Able, the systems analyst, Baker, the network specialist, Charlie, the financial manager, Danny, the IT techie, Evelyn, the support administrator, Francine, the accounts manager, and Goosen, the "humour man", a very positive sales executive who has sold practically everything and achieved every target he was given. His motto was "There's heaven in success selling and joke telling".

When Peter assembled them together, they were very keen to find out their roles in the new business, although their department heads and superiors were very reluctant to get them involved. Each of them has been a key operator in their area. Losing them would affect the sales, the expertise and the support badly needed. However, Peter told them that in the long-term interests of the company, they had better second them initially for the project and then release them once the business was started. There were some objections that he was taking away the best talent from all the divisions, but Peter managed to persuade them that he was not taking away the best but only the most potentially talented in the future company.

As they knew Peter could deliver to the company and he had good relationships with them, they agreed to second them to the project first. The project team reminded him of the film "Magnificent Seven" when Yul Brynner who acted as the leader went to choose 7 persons to fight the bandits in the wild, wild west, Peter has to wage a war against the competitors. All the project team members were flattered to be included in the team, but for some, there were some clashes of priorities. Francine was about to get married and this new venture would be very demanding on her partner. Charlie has just embarked on an MBA study and the demand from both sides would not be able to generate the best from him. Danny has just got a new baby and this was keeping him busy. Personally, Peter was also tight for time with Elizabeth, who has been feeling neglected from time to time.

"Well, ladies and gentlemen, the time is never ideal. We will always be faced with challenging personal circumstances and work demands. However, the opportunity is now here. All these may produce conflicts. That's call 'Life'! Think, and let's vote". 7 finally voted "Yes"!

34   The Professional Networker ~ The System Works!

Tom was glad that despite his absence, his two prospects, William and Henry came to the business opportunity meeting. Paul was waiting for them and introduced himself to them. Quickly, Paul apologised on Tom's behalf that Tom was held back in the office and would they join him in the business preview meeting.

After the meeting, Paul took Willian and Henry aside and asked them questions. "Is there anything said during the meeting that would interest you in pursuing this opportunity?". Paul then kept silent. Half- a-minute passed. A less experienced networking person would then speak and clarified the question, or went on to other aspects of the meeting. Finally, William spoke, "Well, this is nothing new; I have attended similar meetings before." "What about you Henry?", Paul turned to Henry. "Well, I was not sure how the income was calculated? You mean that if I were to pursue this, I can play golf every day of my life?". Paul caught on to this hint, and said," Would you like to play golf every day? Not only on weekends, but also during the weekdays? Mondays, Tuesdays, Wednesdays," Before Paul could even continue, he saw Henry nodding his head in an affirmative way. "Why don't we sit down here and let me show you how this could be realized?"

Paul showed the calculations and how in recruiting 6 members who were active, and how each of them similarly show the concept to 3 others, and then in turn to 2 others, Henry could earn as much as $200,000 per annum, provided each member were to switch each buying behaviour from the supermarket to the electronic catalogue, via the internet. Products would be delivered to the house. Paul warned them that it was not an easy business, but it could lead to Henry being able to play golf in all the beautiful resorts he saw in the presentations. William started to show some interest too as he initially saw it as a "soap and products selling part-time small-income activity", not a "dream realization huge-income and freedom opportunity", and it could be done very professionally and in high self-esteem. Nobody would question him if he were driving an expensive car whether he is a "distributor'? They would in fact admire him as a successful businessman. He never saw the presentation in that way before.

Paul then asked the closing questions, "Why don't both of you become members and explore what the business is really like? you will meet very successful businessman in this network. Many are high-ranking corporate executives and self-employed professionals who have a dream they would like to realize". Both paid the membership fees and signed the forms.

34   The Corporate Executive ~ The System Works!

Able, Baker, Charlie, Danny, Evelyn, Francine, and Goosen. The team members' names sounded something like in the army, especially the first three. Peter could not hide his smile as he thought how coincidence has made this team quite a humorous group to work with, especially Goosen was there. Whenever there was a tough moment, Goosen would suggest something relevant but humorous, and the team would laugh off the tension between members. This diffused many conflicts in the group. Peter now told them how tough this assignment as outsourcing means that they have to burn their bridges and he would like to hear from them their concerns as many have family dependants, and being cast off without a job should the assignment not succeed, would not go well with them. On the other hand, Peter also pointed out the bright future for them if they were to do well. They would be VPs and senior VPs, and even CEOs of their respective niches if the outsourcing worked.

Discussions ensued about the viability of the program, especially since many were fearful of their future. Peter knew that if he could persuade them, they would be able to bring in others with full commitment to the program. Arnold, the CEO, told them to burn their bridges while offering his support to make sure the program worked, otherwise he would be casting away some of the best people in the company. Peter laid down the cards. There would be risks, but there were also successes. One by one, the members signed on the program. Goosen said that he would prefer to be known as the senior VP of humour, rather than salesman of humour, as the former sounded better, even if he had no job should the job failed. "No negatives!" they all shouted at him in jest. With them, Peter got his team.

Peter then met up with April to bounce off his ideas off her, before both met up with Arnold. Arnold was keen that the outsourcing takes place as soon as possible. To make sure that Peter had a base of customers so that outsourcing could start off properly, he suggested that Xylec's and Com-Com be the first two customers of iOutsouce, the name of the new company. Immediately, the staff in the network and IT support functions and jobs would be spun off to this new company. Charges by the month would be made to Xylec and Com-Com, however, the condition being that the total charges should be at least 10%

lower than the current charges, however they were measured.

Based on the quick revenue estimates that Charlie and Francine could work out, iOutsource, would have a gross revenue of $120 million. Therefore, Peter has one year to be financially independent. He is now the interim CEO, to prove his worth.

35   The Professional Networker ~ Core Group!

For Tom, the priority now was to get enough leaders in his organisation. Although he has recruited a large number of frontline members, he knew that only 3 out of 20 would be actively seriously building their network. Right now, he has only one active leader under him who is building his network, although he has many others who tried to build but stalled and has some downlines, and growth was either slow or did not have enough momentum. Although he tried to be the leader by example, the frontlines were not the right people. Paul always told him that he should not try to make leaders of people but choose people who are or want to be leaders. He was also looking for leaders who were teachable, able to follow set plans, rather than try to be too innovative, yet ambitious to choose financial freedom. He had many corporate people who joined him after show them the concept of the business model how they could achieve financial freedom. However, many felt that the method of doing it was too rigid, and became inactive after a few tries. Most complained about the many meetings they had to attend. There were the weekly meetings, then the monthly functions and the quarterly leadership seminars.

Tom wanted to secure two more active leaders among his frontlines so that he could achieve the next level, called the Emerald level, which would have three stable groups of direct distributors who are able to achieve stability in terms of product sales and people building the network, with him helping them to achieve the two objectives. There were two potential, Michael and Julie, who were professional couples, and Joshua, a bachelor, about to marry his classmate sweetheart. They were shown the plan, but somehow had not made the decision to join and work the business. Tom did however follow up on them for three weeks in a row, meeting them thrice, once a week. He suggested that they work out where they see themselves in 5 years' time, the opportunity to be free versus another 20 years of employment. Both the prospects were keen on the idea but kept postponing the sign-up. On the last week, Tom told them why not try the system for 6 months and see if it worked for them. If not, they have nothing to lose, and they would be able to get refund for the membership. With that they agreed and Tom lent them scores of tapes to educate them and to motivate them. Tom also sold them the tickets for the Business Building Seminar.

That convinced them to start on the business. Hopefully, Tom thought he now has his core group that he could build his Emerald level network. It would not be easy to work on three groups at the same time, but this was the best opportunity to move up to the next level. Michael & Julie, Joshua and Kenneth would be his key leaders that he would help to grow their businesses.

35   The Corporate Executive ~ The Core Group!

Peter worked well with his group of 7 people. Each person knew exactly his or her function, and recruited the type of people each person was looking for, that could work hard, and contribute to the group. No one slackened and they all worked very late to bring the company into full operation. Initially there were some intense communications and coordination between Xylec, Com-Com and iOutsource as staff transferred over, and new staff joined the group. Because people had to resign from their company and take up new contractual employments with iOutsource, there were some hesitancies. As the company progressed and the new employment terms came to be known as more attractive, with the risks, iOursource even had to be more selective in taking employees in.

Each senior VP had the right to designate his or her new title, and there was much fun. One of them called himself the Commander of the Network Operations, instead of the more mundane Senior VP of Network Operations. It was flexibility like this which endeared many to the new company. The core group of seven together determined the culture of the new company, which was to be objective oriented but fun to work in, little bureaucracy and operations oriented, serving the clients efficiently, at the best cost and with innovative packaging. There was nothing they could not form contractual relationships with clients. As Peter was quite easy to work with as long as the bottom-line results were met, the core group team relished the freedom to chart their own course, as long as the company wide objectives were met.

Charlie and Francine were very good with the accounting and financial systems they set up. Able, Baker, Danny, Evelyn, and Goosen were responsible for the marketing and technical setup, together with simple processes that could fix almost any outsourcing needs of clients, whether internal or external. With the support from the Xylec and Com-Com, they started to market to the fifty of the largest corporations in the nation that had extensive communications and networks that could be outsourced. The board room was full of proposals, budgets, costings and discussions how to win over customers. There were also partnerships with technology partners like IBM, Sun Microsystems, HP and Oracle that could market together with their clients.

IBM was also an outsourcing company, so it also a competitor and also partner as iOutsource could work as an extension of IBM's outsourcing contracts. In addition to this, iOutsource hired many contract workers for the outsourcing clients that it had already at hand. The seven-core group were wonderful with the best teamwork.

36   The Professional Networker ~ One Quit.

Tom had three active groups sponsoring and being active in the business. The other frontlines were less active and had less people. Then one of the group leaders quit because of personal reasons; he could not keep up the pace of the business as his spouse was not active in the business and felt neglected. This led to frequent quarrel with the wife threatening to separate from him if he did not quit as he was spending so much time in the evenings. One day he told Tom he needed to counsel with him. That was when Tom was told that that his marriage was more important to him right now rather than have future time and income. They have tried in the past to interest the wife in the business, but she was more interested in spending time and recreation with her husband. Now that she was unable to do it and became very resentful. That came to a row when she saw Tom with one of his downlines, a lady, driving to a prospect's house and they appeared to be enjoying themselves. After analysing all the possibilities, Tom told his frontline that maybe he should lie low for a while. Tom would look after his group.

However, his group was more familiar with him rather than Tom, and his downlines started to focus back on their families. This started a chain reaction, which led one after another quitting the business until the whole group had less than 3 active persons. Tom learned his lesson to have more spare legs or groups so that he would not have to depend on this particular leg to move up to the Emerald level. Tom was very disappointed that a leg could be so fragile. He sought counsel with Paul

Paul listened to Tom and encouraged. "This is quite common, because the number of people resigning will always happen. You have to show more plans so that more people will join than resign.

With this momentum, you will have growth. If more people resign than join, your group's growth will slow down. Another thing is that you must work at the newest person in the active group yourself so that they will identify you as the upline who's helping them. If you help enough people to achieve what they want, you will be able to achieve whatever you want. This is something familiar which the founder of the network has stated before. The next thing is that you need to have more legs or groups, so that you work with the best three groups, and not with only three groups.

That way, you have freedom to cultivate more than three group leaders as your leaders to take to the next level, that is to direct distributor level where they will have a stable income each of over $50,000 per year, and you will be able to be an Emerald, earning over $80,000 per year. Learn from your experience and you build the biggest business this way". Tom understood.

36   The Corporate Executive ~ One Quit.

Danny, the IT techie, had been pushing his efforts to build up the team so that it has the technology and the most outstanding people in network that the town could buy. However, one day, he called to take emergency leave as he has to send his mother to hospital. Over the next few days, he was very quiet and moody which prompted Goosen to joke that "hey, where did you leave your moods, in the hospital?". With that Danny snapped and yelled at Goosen, "Watch your tongue, will you!", and this surprised everybody. As everyone stared at Danny, and he left the room, Goosen ran after him and apologised. They were in deep discussion. When Goosen returned, he told the rest of the team, "Danny's leaving the team…his mother is not well. She is dying!" The rest of the team were in deep shock. Danny was always the more devoted to the project as he was always interested in techie things. He would always bring in new equipment, parts that were never seen in the market yet, and he would spend hours after office trying to figure out how to work the items. Peter learned that Danny was very devoted to his mother who had encouraged him on computers and those electronics. She has been diagnosed with leukemia, and has only a few more months to leave. Danny has asked to resign to care for his mother. Peter granted him indefinite leave.

Without Danny, the network solutions were held back a bit as he was the best. His technical programming and knowledge of connectivity with equipment was unchallenged. Now that he is not available, and the business was growing by twofold, it was proving a strain on the team to bring all the outsourcing solutions together. But somehow or rather, the team managed, and when they were stuck, Danny would be consulted by phone. At times, he would pop in. Six months later, the team learned the bad news. Danny's mother passed away. They arranged to attend the funeral. Danny was really emotionally down.

Days and weeks passed. Danny showed up one day, and requested to meet Peter. Danny was no longer his former self. He was very downcast. He told Peter he could no longer work in iOutsourcing and needed time to recover. He wanted to travel to a town in France, where his mother met his father.

He had to see the place where love blossomed into a family of which Danny was part. He was not sure how long he would be there. He felt sorry that he had to leave the team because he could not keep the company waiting for him. He wanted to quit.

Peter could not hold back Danny. He has to now search for one more member that would make it back to the 'Magnificent Seven".

37   The Professional Networker ~ The Search Begins...

Tom began to show more plans to find his next few leaders. Plan after plan, he could not identify persons that he could develop as leaders. Initially, the people he was looking for must have the vision of seeking freedom. He realised how many were very contented in their jobs, even with the lower income than they could get from the networking business and the even less disposable time they are given. He saw more than 20 persons, some of which joined but it was strange, that at least three would begin to work on the network. However, not all was able to build a bigger network. Some just wanted to be customers, signing on as members to take advantage of the discount given as distributors.

Then one day, it happened as he met up with 30 more persons. Forty of them in total said no to the opportunity but 10 joined. Of these, two had potentially very strong reasons to build the business. One of them, Colin, had struggled all his life; he supported himself on part-time jobs to pay his tuition fees for school and for college. Now working as an engineer, his pay was never enough for his aim to own a house so that he and his mother and siblings could stay together. When he say the opportunity, he did not hesitate to ask, "what must I do to be a successful diamond and entrepreneur?". He asked a lot of sensible questions on income, the network and how to bring people to functions, which was the key to a successful networking business. The other person that Peter thought was smart and sharp was Amrik. An IT professional, he was tired of the long hours he had to spend in his firm and wanted to have more time with his family, His wife did not have a full-time paid job but had to forgo her job to look after their one-year-old son. As this network business allowed her to earn extra income and spend more time with her husband, both were very enthusiastic about the business.

Tom spent evenings with these two new members. Colin was the more receptive to ideas and although he asked lots of questions, the moment he was satisfied with the answers, he worked on the network business without looking back. Amrik and wife were also good listeners and asked the right questions. However, they always were looking at ways how to better improve the technique in showing plans, and devised their own way of drawing in new members.

Although they had new distributors, many did not follow the system, as a result of which, everyone was doing their own thing. There was little duplication of the activities done, and Tom had to help them undo many things with their downlines. As a result, Colin progressed faster, and built up his building blocks of business faster. Tom knew he had his third leader.

37   The Corporate Executive ~ The Search Begins…

Peter spread word that he was looking for a replacement for Danny. It was not easy. Many candidates were met but because the team had Danny as the model, the search was not successful. Peter then had to resort to using professional search firms, the "head-hunters" who would identify, locate and persuade the candidate to try for Danny's position. The fee for such a search was not low and it was about 30% of the gross annual income, which includes the basic income, the bonuses, allowances, fringe benefits such as company car and paid annual leave. The fee alone would be about $100,000 for a successful search assignment. Finally, he changed his candidate specifications, and one potential person, Eric, was called in for interview.

Eric was brilliant in network technology, communications technology and technical programming, but his people skills were a bit short. He would look at a person without saying anything or exchanging a greeting, but went straight to the problem. Many times, the team who also took part in the recruitment process, was taken aback by the abrupt questions and answers from Eric. None of the other candidates was as good technically as Eric, although overall, there were a few candidates who were better. The team met with Peter and a vote was called for. Three voted to recruit Eric but three voted against. Peter had the deciding casting vote. He made his call to hire Eric, but he would address Eric.

Before he made the financial offer to Eric, Peter spoke to him candidly that his people skills could be improved. Eric told him bluntly, "Do you want me for my technical wizardry or for my people skills?", and remained silent. Peter was taken back by his question. He thought deeply over this question and then smiled broadly, "Of course, both if you can. If not, could you learn?". Eric without smiling replied," Of course. Any specific area you could identify for me?" Peter almost fell off his chair, but kept his restraint, and said, "Yes, everything about human relations and people skills. Here, I have two book which I think you should read". Peter gave him, "Skills with People" by Les Giblin and "How to Win Friends and Influence People" by Dale Carnegie. Eric took the book and grinned finally, "So Simple? Of course,". Peter shook Eric's hand and welcomed him into the team.

Peter 's team was now back to seven. It was similar to the movie, "Dirty Dozen", which was about a movie of commandos, each skilled differently, but one was slightly less than normal. Peter hoped that Eric would solve his team's problems without upsetting anyone in the team.

38   The Professional Networker ~ Going Emerald

Tom set his goals with the counselling of Paul. Paul probed Tom with soul searching questions. What did Tom really want out of this business? What date to achieve financial freedom and free constraints of time? What were the 100 things he wanted out of his life? Tom had written his goals and objectives. The difficulty was setting down the date. If he were to put it down to early, he might not achieve it and he will become disappointed. If too far away, it might not seem possible. Paul told him the dates and goals were important, but what was more important, was his decision to really go for the goal. That decision was what he needed to tell his heart he is ready. Many people have not set goals and objectives. Nor have they decided. So, attaining the goal was not achievable. When a person gets married, they just do it because they decided. Then dates are set. In a similar manner, Paul suggested Tom decide and then fix a date.

Tom went back and discussed with Shirley. They looked at the organisation of distributors. Three active groups, with many half-active groups, and one back-up group just in case. One group had all the vital signs, meaning they had the desired frontlines, the number of downlines, the number of people attending the monthly and the quarterly functions. In addition, there were the desired number of people who subscribed to the books and tapes to enrich and broaden their minds, learn about business building techniques and be motivated. The second and third group need to add further frontlines and downlines, and attain the desired numbers to match the vital signs. With three groups reaching the maximum business volume, then Tom could reach the Emerald status if all the three groups qualified in one year with at least 6 months of such volume.

After much thought and discussion, Tom set the date of 31 December as his target date. It was now January and he gave himself 12 months to build up the business and for his three leaders to become direct distributors. This needed 6 months. Paul met up with Tom. With a shrug of his shoulder, Tom told Paul the date. After checking on the vital signs, and further discussion each of the groups, and the other legs, Paul congratulated Tom for the decision and Pual promised to help Tom to achieve the goal.

This was a goal that required teamwork and Paul would help to pull the group up based on his experience in building his own group to be an Emerald. Now to work on it.

38   The Corporate Executive ~ Going for the Top Five.

Peter already set the target to be the among the top 5 firms in computer network operating systems, servers, network administration, wireless and wired communications network. A network connects two or more computers so that they can share information, applications or resources. Cisco is one of the top firms in this area. It has connectivity, architecture, infrastructure, protocols, security and storage. However, iOutsource plan is to be among top 5 firms in the industry for outsourcing. To do this, Peter knew his firm must be known to all the top industry, service and government groups, which means good marketing and lobbying of sales and services.

39   Real People and Scenario Behind the Stories

We come to the end of the stories. The people and scenario described are based on true events.

Some professional networkers have achieved their goals as Amway Diamonds and upper levels of the professional marketing network and hierarchy. They have continuous income and travel yearly on paid vacations. Their lifestyle is enviable and many have chosen this path.

The corporate executives have also achieved their goals as CEOs, Presidents, or even Chairman of companies through their shrewd work and associations with companies, founders and corporate chiefs.

These are the tale of two choices. Interesting and rewarding for those who make it.

This book is written to motivate and inspire people going into the world.

Good luck and good venture.

www.ingramcontent.com/pod-product-compliance
Lightning Source LLC
Chambersburg PA
CBHW071208240526

45470CB00018B/1595